BRUSHSTROKES
OF LIFE:
An Autobiography

to RANDY & LYN

xoy

MYRTLE-ANNE REMPEL

ISBN 978-1-64114-176-5 (paperback)
ISBN 978-1-64114-177-2 (digital)

Christian Faith Publishing, Inc.
832 Park Avenue
Meadville, PA 16335
www.christianfaithpublishing.com

Printed in the United States of America

Foreword

My career for the most part of my working life was as a Visual Artist after graduating from the University of the Fraser Valley in 1986. My studio was in the loft of our Penthouse in Abbotsford. I spent many hours creating pieces of art of which I received many awards for my work.

Ed used to lie on the sofa in our Great Room when he started to get sick. I could look down at him from my studio and I could see when he became restless. I would come down to attend to him and then go back to my studio, but found that my paints had all dried up, and that the passion for the work that I was doing had subsided.

I decided to take a hiatus from my painting and concentrate on writing a book about our lives, which I had always wanted to do. I could do this on my computer near Ed and also keep watch over him.

In this little story, I will try to capture the essence of who we were and how we lived our lives. It is a synoptic of stories that I wanted to record for my family and friend for years to come.

I am so grateful to all of you for encouraging me to write these memories. I hope I can, in a small way, help you to gain the strength you need to endure some of the battles that you face also.

I recently read a quote which I really like.

"By God's grace, may we make each day our masterpiece for Him"—David McCasland.

CHAPTER 1

Beginnings

I was born in Swift Current, Saskatchewan, and grew up with six younger brothers and no sisters.

My parents met in Saskatchewan when my mom was working on a farm as a housekeeper when my dad came through to work on the Dalgetty farm too. My mom was engaged to marry the owner's son, but fell in love with my father so broke off her engagement and decided to marry Bill Reimer, my father.

My mother was from a very different background than my father. I think they both only had about grade six and eight educations. It was in the Depression years and Dad rode the boxcars to find work on various farms.

My grandparents lived in Herbert Sask where my grandparents attended the Mennonite Conference church.

After my parents got engaged, they planned a wedding in the church. My mom sewed a beautiful long satin gown and had a lovely veil to go along with it. However, she found out she was pregnant before the wedding, and the church refused to let her get married in it so they had a simple wedding in my grandparents' home without a veil being worn.

My aunt Lou told me this story about ten or twelve years ago. My mom lost the baby shortly after they married. I was surprised to hear this, as I thought I was her first pregnancy.

My grandparents, the Doerksens, were from Russia and immigrated to Canada in 1926 to 1927. I knew that grandfather was originally from the Netherlands and he had previously worked in a flourmill in Russia. Before he came to Canada, my grandfather, Jacob R. Doerksen, had been married earlier, and had two children. Later, after his wife died, he then married my grandmother, Agatha Krause, who was ten years younger than he was. Before they immigrated to the prairies in Canada, they endured much hardship, famine, and violence. I will leave it to others to tell of their history and their life in Russia.

I think they did farming in the prairies of Saskatchewan, but moved to Abbotsford, British Columbia, in approximately 1946. They had twelve children, of whom nine survived—Jake, Mary, Annie, Ike, Abe, Katherine (my mom), Sarah, Louise, and Johnnie. My grandmother raised her stepchildren just like her own and we considered them our uncle and his children our cousins.

My father had a slightly more colorful background. His father (my grandfather) came from Poland in the early 1900s. There is some speculation that he was given the name Reimer when he arrived in Canada. When he lived in Canada, he married three times. He had a large family, living in Swift Current, many of whom were successful farmers. He divorced his first wife, married another lady and divorced again, and had no children.

He then married my grandmother, Anne Ubel. Before they moved to Swift Current, they had three children—Pauline, who lived in Manitoba all her life; George, who married a few times; and William (Bill), who was born in Whitemouth, Manitoba on March 1912

My grandfather Stanley and grandmother Anne separated and he went off to Vancouver, British Columbia, to live.

So, by then, my parents, who were living in Swift Current, kindly had grandmother Anne come to live with them. She died shortly after that but when I was born in 1937, she really wanted my parents to name me Myrtle-Anne. My mom had decided on Marilyn, but deferred to my grandmother's wishes.

Bill and Kate (my mom) had a busy life as it was during the war and the Depression. My dad was not conscripted into the war, because had a huge chest deformity. The only childhood memento he possessed was a Confirmation Certificate from the Lutheran church when he was confirmed as a child.

When Bill's parents divorced (or separated), my parents moved to Swift Current, and Dad worked hauling water and ice for the city. He worked very hard for his growing family. He later was a mechanic on airplanes, and worked as a mechanic in a car dealership. He quickly rose to be a foreman.

When they moved to Swift Current, and after me, they had, Ronald Lawrence, Eugene Donald, Murray James, Gordon William, Roger Alan, and lastly Keith Raymond.

My brother Gordon and Roger are only eleven months apart, and when Roger was born, I remember my mom feeding him with an eye dropper, fashioning an incubator in a drawer, and putting hot water bottles around him to keep him warm, as he was only a little over three pounds. She used to pinch him to get him to drink. Because they were close in age, Gordon and Roger became good buddies growing up.

Keith was born three years later and I was disappointed that he was not a girl. I really wanted a sister, but it was not to be. My parents had seven children in ten years. My mom would say that Bill would just drop his pants, and she would be pregnant. Gordon was the only child born at home. All the rest of us were born in the Swift Current Hospital.

There was a couple living in Swift Current who couldn't have children and desperately wanted to adopt Keith, but my parents were adamant that Keith would always be their son.

This couple owned the Lux Theater in Swift Current, and my brothers and I would often be allowed to go to a show there. I think it cost five cents but Gene always got in free. If films with Roy Rogers, Gene Autry, or Lassie came to town, we were ecstatic to be able to go.

I felt we had a wonderful childhood. As I was the only girl, my dad, who was one of the handiest and most hardworking man I knew, built a shed in the backyard and he let me use it as a playhouse. The boys had the whole yard to play in. My two girlfriends, Shannon Nelson and Janice Atkinson, and I had lots of fun as young girls playing in there. Our yard was large and the boys and I played "kick the can" and numerous other games.

Before my father built the house we lived in; we had lived in rental places. I remember one place where we had a "peeping Tom" that my mom and Aunt Lou would always tell my dad about when he was away at work. I was so frightened of this person, whomever he was.

Our new home had a front porch (veranda). I spent many hours playing there with my very first doll that I received when I was about six or seven years old. It was the most precious thing I had ever seen. My mom handmade clothes for my doll.

The house had two stories and a basement. The boys slept upstairs (which was unfinished) and had just two by fours separating the room. I slept in a small space downstairs, as did my parents and baby Keith.

I vaguely remember the year 1945. There was a huge celebration on the streets and parades and bands playing everywhere. Everyone was so happy. I was told the war was over, which I didn't know much about, other than that my uncles were conscripted to serve.

One of my uncles, Tommy, had his leg blown off in the war. He was married to my Aunt Mary. They had one son, George, much later in life.

When I was quite young, my parents let me go to Regina, where Aunt Mary and Uncle Tommy lived. Because at that time they didn't have any children, they totally spoiled me. They had the most beautiful china cabinet in their apartment, with all kind of pretty, colorful items in it. I had never seen anything like it. They both worked for the city of Regina, and I thought they much be so very rich. I think I developed the joy of collecting colorful glass items then.

Our home in Swift Current was quite bare, with just the most essential items that we needed. My mother hand sewed and made most of all our clothes, with underwear made from flour sacks. She was fastidious about cleanliness, which was hugely important to her. She would scrub the flours, polish them, and we would sit on the mop while she pulled us around to shine the floors.

My aunts, Sarah and Lou, spent a lot of time in at my parents' home because they were attending business schools. They spoiled me, and one day my aunt Lou painted my fingernails. They were so pretty and I felt so special.

My brother Gordon was the only one born at home. Aunt Lou was there when my mom gave birth in a hurry. He still says that he has never stayed in a hospital.

The rest of us were born in the hospital. It was important for us to have good health and I remember the cod-liver-oil spoon, which we all got, and the weekly baths in hand boiled water and the visits to the dentist. We all got our tonsils taken out one month. Three of us at a time, and then the other three kids the next month. I guess they thought that was really important as my dad had a really bad infection in his tonsils one year and was really sick. Keith was too young then.

My father had never had a Christmas or birthday gift given to him. His table manners were poor. My mom had been from a generous family, so when she did not get a Christmas gift from him, she was so disappointed. He soon learned that these traditions were very important and became very generous.

Our gifts at Christmas were very simple. One year we got a pencil with an eraser on the end, which was rare at that time. Another year, I heard him sawing and pounding in the basement, but we were not allowed to go down there to see what was happening. We thought he was just finishing something for the house. It turned out to be a little footstool with a slot in the top to carry it. Each one that he made for us older kids was painted a different color. I thought it was really nice, and so special.

One year we had our photos taken for a family picture. I was wearing a dress that my parents gave me for Christmas. It was my first "bought" dress, but I hated it, and cried when I opened the box. It was maroon with white piping on it. What an ungrateful kid I was!

My earliest recollection was of the fun time my brothers and I had while visiting our cousins on a farm near Herbert Sask. Because we always lived in the center of the city of Swift Current, we had many fun times on our cousins' farm in that area.

My girl cousins, Emily and Lillian, lived there. Their father was twenty years older than their mother, and a wealthy bachelor farmer when he met my aunt. Because he was so much older and more accomplished, he was very strict with his family.

I remember many fun times in the fields playing with pieces of grain and us girls fashioning dolls out of the grain. We got bits of rags and pretended they were clothes. One day, Lillian and Emily and I wore gorgeous white dresses that our moms made. They had red piping on them, and I was so proud to have a beautiful dress like the other girls.

On another day, I was invited to stay on the farm with the family for the weekend. Their house was large and totally immaculate. The banister and stairs had to be polished every day, and if Uncle Martin inspected them and they were not perfect, we would get into trouble. I remember that the lights always had to be turned off when we left a room and every door had to be closed tightly. On reflection now, I think that it was probably to preserve the heat in the home.

Because they were farmers and had hired help working there, the meals that my aunt prepared were big and sumptuous, especially breakfast. I was used to my mom making a big pot of porridge, either Sunny Boy Cereal or oatmeal, or a variation of that. Here at the farm, there were large meals of eggs, sausages, bacon, potatoes, and many other things. I could not possibly eat that amount of food.

We were told that we could not leave the table until our plates were empty. We must be grateful, as there were so many people in the world starving, and we should not waste food. We were also not allowed to talk at the table at all. My cousins and I would giggle sometimes, but my uncle's stern looks soon stopped that. But my aunt gently reassured me that I was okay. I was very frightened.

I remember a time there when the youngest member of their family died as a baby. I think his name was Clifford. Now it would be called a crib death, but then it was classified as poor care of a baby. It was an incredibly sad time for that family. I heard about the funeral for their wee baby and it was the first time that I had ever experienced mourning over a death.

During one of those summers when I was five and a half years old, my brother Eugene, who was two years younger than I was, fell and could not get up. He was later diagnosed with infantile paralysis (polio).

My mother was a dear. Because Eugene (whom we all called Gene) was too ill to go to children's hospital in Winnipeg, and so contagious, she kept him isolated in the living room with herself only and put hot compresses on his limbs night and day.

There was a huge epidemic in Swift Current before the vaccine was discovered. He had infantile paralysis and when he was well enough, he was transported to Winnipeg, where he was in an iron lung until the paralysis left him with paralysis only from the hip down on one leg. Initially he was paralyzed from the neck down. He was such a brave soul and came home after some time with a brace and special shoes on one leg as well as crutches.

It was amazing that none of our family got this disease, a tribute to my mom's fastidious cleanliness and diligence. It is also amazing that she did not contract the disease. Because our home was quarantined, I was not able to start school that fall and had to wait another year.

Gene suffered greatly with numerous operations but never fell behind in a year in school.

My dad bought a wagon, and Ron pulled Gene around in that. When he was older, my dad bought Ron a bike so that he could take Gene to school on it. We were not allowed to ride it, as it was so precious to the family.

The kids at school were not nice to him and would often push him down as he tried to walk with his crutches.

Later on in high school, after we moved to Abbotsford, he became the envy of all the kids, as he took weightlifting and later became a world-class hero, winning over one hundred medals in Pan-

American and Para-Olympic games. He later had a school named after him and also received an honorary doctorate of laws from the University of the Fraser Valley. He has his name and many medals in the BC Sports Hall of Fame, the National Sports Hall of Fame, as well as in the Abbotsford Hall of Fame.

A funny incident happened one summer. Fresh fruit was scarce in our home because it was during the war years.

One day, when Murray, Ron, and Gene were playing a few blocks away, one of the guys broke the storekeeper's window and stole some apples or an orange. The shopkeeper saw them and chased after the boys but couldn't catch them. However, they had left Gene in the wagon there. Next thing you know, the shopkeeper came to our home pulling Gene in the wagon. My father was so outraged. First he had to pay for the window and then he had to deal with the boys.

Ron always seemed to get the worst of the belt when Dad disciplined the boys, as he was the oldest, but this time, Daddy (as we always called him) told the boys to take off all their clothes other than their undershorts. He said he had phoned the police and they were coming to pick up all three boys and put them in striped uniforms that the prisoners wore and would be put in jail. I don't think I have ever seen such scared and contrite boys for all this day and night. He said, "No point on putting on clothes. They would just have to take them off." I don't think our family ever stole another thing in their lives.

My aunties Sarah (we called her Sadie or sometimes Sade) and Lou visited us really often. They sometimes stayed with us during the week, as they both were in business school. As the war was on then, both of them met dashing young men. Lou met Len Lloyd and she got married to him. He had many illnesses and surgeries due to injuries he received in the war. Later on, they moved a lot in Alberta, as he got a great job as a health inspector with the province of Alberta. Lou was working in an insurance office. They only had one child, Judy.

My school years, my mom did my hair in either French braids or ringlets. In grade three, there were four sets of twins in my class.

Two sets of identical twin girls, one set of fraternal twin girls, and one set of a boy and a girl. I heard at that time that this was quite unusual.

Just about the time, when I was about eleven years old, I went to a service at a church in the neighborhood. My parents never went to church but that evening I heard that God loved me and that if I would give my heart to Him, that I would become a Christian. I went forward and prayed the prayer. The lady counseling me said that I needed to tell someone what I did. I didn't know much about this whole thing.

I was so afraid to tell my parents, that I just shook, but finally I told my mom. She said that I needed to tell my daddy, and now I was very fearful. When I told him, he just smiled and said, "That's nice." I was so relieved that I was not going to be punished.

I read the little book that the church lady gave me. Later I heard that my parents gave their hearts to God a few months later and decided that they needed to start a new life at the coast of BC.

They were both smokers and drank quite a bit, especially my father. Christmas was always fun, but my daddy always drank too much on Christmas Eve and would be sick on Christmas Day.

My parents used to have a lot of parties at our house, because they had all the kids, so on the weekends when us kids were all asleep, they would have lots of friends over. My dad and his buddies would play poker on Saturday nights.

I remember hearing the noise from downstairs one evening, so I crept down sitting on the step, and my mom asked me if I wanted to lick out the whipped cream bowl. I had never tasted anything so wonderful. That was the first time I had that as a child.

My mom left my dad once when I was about seven years old. It was only a week, but my aunt came over to look after us for a bit. I remember being very hungry one day, because there was no food in the house except for a block of cheese. I didn't even know what it was, but ate it. My parents reconciled and she came home.

Even though we did not have much money in Saskatchewan, my father built a nice home, one of four homes that he built, three of which were in Abbotsford.

My parents later decided if they wanted to change their lives, they should move to a different environment so they sold their home, sold everything, and bought a new Chevy coupe, put two-year-old Keith's crib on the top, put food and clothes in the trunk, and made their way to the coast with all us kids in the car.

My mom was so frightened of the mountains that she vowed that she would never go back over that road again in the future. She had lived on the prairies her whole life. We left Swift Current in 1949 and moved to Abbotsford, British Columbia.

I remember that we did stop in a motel one night, absolutely exhausted and tired of traveling. My mom always made lunches for us on the way with food she kept in the trunk.

I am amazed to this day how they managed to travel so lightly. I think they may have sold everything in Swift Current.

It was not that pleasant traveling with nine people in a coupe car. Ron and I had to care for Gordon and Roger on our knees or between us. Of course, Murray, who was always rambunctious, got into a lot of trouble teasing us.

My mom Katie Reimer.

My brothers and I before Keith was born.
Back Row, Ron, Myrtle-Anne, Murray
Front Row, Roger, Eugene & Gordon.

Parents Wedding Picture.

CHAPTER 2

Abbotsford Days

We stopped in Calgary to visit my uncle Ike and aunt Bernice and Darlene and her baby brother, Glen. Dad thought about settling there but didn't find a job he liked.

My uncle was so much fun, and used to come around the corner, and scare us and say, "Boo!" My brothers and I always ended up calling him Uncle Boo. My cousin Darlene (then Doerksen) and I became close and she became a bridesmaid at my wedding to Ed later in life.

When we arrived in Abbotsford, which is where my Doerksen grandparents lived, my dad got a job at Brenner Motors as head mechanic. He later left that and bought some service stations. My brothers helped him with pumping gas on the weekends and my dad did heavy-duty mechanic work.

All my brothers, and I think myself also, are good business people and I think we got that from my dad. We got our hard work ethic from my mom. They were both very intelligent.

My grandparents lived in this little house, on the corner of Old Yale Road and Clearbrook Road. They had fruit trees in the back. My parents were so impressed with the fruit trees, and especially the plum tree in the backyard. My mother would gather the plums and make jam and a sweet soup out of them.

I remember many fond memories of my grandparents. Their little house was immaculate and always smelled of good food. Every time we would come, she would take my brothers and I downstairs to a huge room called the pantry. She would let us choose cookies and other goodies. It was quite something.

The home had a huge grandfather clock in the living room and there was never any music, so all you could here was the loud noises of the clock.

My dad had always cut all my brothers' hair since they were little. So, my grandfather would ask him to trim his white beard and cut his hair. Every week, my dad would do this and if we came along, we were rewarded with good treats. He always would ask my dad to wind the big clock. He was a kindly gentleman who sat in his rocking chair.

My grandmother always crocheted and made little satin quilts. I got some of these gems when I married and when Cheryl was born, she made a lovely little satin quilt of periwinkle blue and rose pink on the other side. It was so beautiful. Cheryl later on used it in her doll carriages.

I grew up in the Abbotsford area and had a wonderful childhood. My brothers and I were quite close in ages, so all my girlfriends would come over to my parents' home, as all my brothers and their friends were there. We did so many fun things together.

Our first home that my parents rented was right across from an old Sikh temple. We had a dirt hill on the property and the boys and I had lots of fun playing on it. One day, I had an unusual thing happen to my body, and felt such shame and fear. I did not know what was happening, and when I told my mom, she just smiled and told me that I was now starting puberty. I had never expected this, as she had never shared this with me.

The house we lived in was pretty old, and as I slept on a couch in the living room, I was kept awake a lot at night with the sound of horrible noises. I was fearful that someone was breaking into our home. My dad later told me it was mice in the walls.

Later on, my dad built a lovely home on Cannon Drive, where I had my own bedroom. It was so nice to have a new home to move into.

The house had a finished basement and the older boys had rooms down there. It had a laundry and a nice recreation room. Keith and I had bedrooms upstairs along with my parents. We lived there until I graduated. The high school was just up the hill from our home.

When we first arrived in Abbotsford, we went off to the airport school, as the other schools in the area were not finished yet. It was an airport hangar. A bus would pick us up and take us there. I was in charge of my three older brothers, Ron, Eugene, and Murray, being sure that they got on it okay for the return home. Ron and I looked everywhere for Murray, and couldn't find him. We were so anxious, but when we returned home, he was there. He had walked home because he didn't like it. I was in grade six, and made wonderful friends. We later went on to Philip Sheffield School.

My parents heard that in Clearbrook, there was a German school. Because none of my siblings could speak German, they thought it would be good for us to learn German. Well, the first day we went, of course we couldn't speak a word, so we were overwhelmed.

When my dad came to pick us up, we told him that they basically "kicked us out" as they said it was just for kids who could speak some German. I guess it was for improving their language skills. My mom could speak some German but my dad could not.

Gene, Ron, and I were happy because we didn't want to go to school on Saturdays anyway. So no one in our family ever learned this language that so many people in Abbotsford could speak. Later on in high school, I took three years of French in my program.

CHAPTER 3

Darlene

My aunt Sarah, as she is called now, married a very handsome, tall, dark-haired man named George Raffle, whom she met and married in Swift Current. They later moved to New Westminster, BC. George was spoiled so he was not very good at working. They had a baby girl named Darlene.

My aunt Sarah had a very good job at the BC telephone company, and worked very hard. One day, while she was at work, George left Darlene outside a pub while he went in to get a drink. My aunt was phoned by the police to come and get Darlene.

My parents then came and got her to stay at our home. She stayed with us during the week for a few years, while Sarah worked and went home with her on the weekends. Sarah and George divorced and Darlene's mom raised her on her own. Sarah was able to buy a house with some guarantees from her brother John, and she and Darlene lived in this home on Sixth Avenue for many years until Darlene grew up and started to work in the telephone company as well.

Darlene was only around two years old when she came to stay at our home. While aunt Sarah worked, Darlene stayed with us.

I loved her like a little sister. I played with her and spoiled her and was so happy to have a little girl in the home. Later on, when Darlene grew up and got married, she lived in West Vancouver, and later married Paul Howard. We are still very good friends and call each other "sis."

Ed and I became guardians of their two boys Christopher and Reid. We were also godparents to Reid.

We get together often even now and I have visited their home in Palm Desert as well.

Darlene recalls that even when I got married and moved away, my mom, who was always very good to her, helped her to get work in the berry plant.

CHAPTER 4

Working

As I said, my parents were hard working and my brothers and I sometimes helped out in the service stations that my parents owned. I remember, that one summer my dad gave me a "balloon tire" bike as payment for pumping gas.

My parents took us kids to White Rock almost every Sunday afternoon in the summer when the weather was nice. I remember so many fun times playing in the sand, building sand castles, watching the tide come in, and eating the wonderful lunches my mom made. We would build a bonfire and roast wieners, and go home so tired and sunburned but so happy.

My parents did fun things with us. One day my daddy said that we all had to get in the car to go to Vancouver as the new bridge had been opened. Before that, one had to go through the Pattullo Bridge in New Westminster to get into the city. Now there was a bridge called the Port Mann. I didn't think much about it being significant, other than it was big, so high, and everyone was blowing their horns going through it, in celebration of it opening.

Many Sunday afternoons, my dad would pack us up in the car and say, "Who wants to go for ice cream?" Off we would go to the Milk Bar in downtown Abbotsford, where we could get a double ice cream cone for six cents. A single was five cents but Daddy said we could have a double. Wow, that was so special.

One weekend, my parents decided to go to Victoria for the day. They only took me and left my brothers with an aunt for the day. This was the only time that I can remember going on a trip alone with my parents. I think I was about twelve years old.

I was awestruck with the beauty of the parliament buildings and the gorgeous parks in Victoria. It was also my first ride on the ferry going over.

I don't know how my dad did it, raising seven kids. My mom never worked outside of the home, and yet we never felt we were poor. My father was far from perfect and had faults, like all of us do, but he was certainly a good provider and loved his family.

As I mentioned earlier, my dad had built a nice home on Cannon Drive in Abbotsford a block away from the Abbotsford Senior High School. I remember that when the first bell would ring, I would just have enough time to run up the hill and make it in time for my first class.

One day my brothers were caught smoking. My dad was so angry. Because he had adult-onset asthma and my mom had hay fever and asthma, he cautioned us not to smoke and try to keep our lungs healthy. He told the boys that they could not do anything worse than that for their health.

Up until then, I picked berries every summer and babysat for people whenever I could for twenty-five cents an hour. I usually had enough money from that to buy school clothes.

One year, I had enough saved to buy a pink cashmere sweater and loved it so much that I'm sure I nearly wore it out along with my "bobby sox" and saddle shoes.

My older brothers and I picked strawberries at the Rempel Farm. Ed was the "Straw Boss." Mr. Rempel used to pick us up in the morning and take us to his farm. Ed used to follow me around, and I heard that if the boss follows you around, you are not picking cleanly, so I tried extra hard.

One day, my brothers Gene, Ron, and Murray were throwing berries at older women in the patch when they bent over. Eddie fired them and told them not to come back.

The next morning, Mr. Rempel came to pick them up, and asked my mom why they weren't ready. When my mom told him that Eddie had fired them, he replied that it was okay. "Boys will be boys," he said.

I don't know how he made much money, as he was always bringing watermelons and revels for treats for us. When it was too hot, he told us that we could go home. We would go swimming in Mill Lake then.

We loved swimming in the lake, which now no one can swim in. It is far too dangerous. Our dad taught us all to swim. I used to go out to the middle of the lake and just lay there, floating, looking at the clouds. I never realized how dangerous that was, as it was an old water lake made up of lots of dead wood, etc., from the mill that used to be there. One day while walking home from the lake which was just a short walk from my home, I saw Ed driving a motorcycle and I waved at him. He gave me a ride home on it. What a thrill that was.

I remember when my dad bought our first TV set. We were all enthralled. Mom and Dad would watch wrestling and the *Ed Sullivan Show*. One day we saw Elvis Presley on the show. It was so thrilling. There were a few movies on, but not much else.

We had a big park across the street and my brothers and Dad would make a baseball diamond on it, with Gene's diamond a lot smaller and he would go around the bases on all four limbs. We had lots of fun there. On the property, there was a swamp and at night we would hear the frogs croaking loudly.

My parents paid for us older kids to get one year of music lessons each from the lady Mrs. Nelson who owned the property. They also bought a piano, and later on Ron a trumpet, Murray a trombone, Gene a sax. The noise from practicing our music in our home was not pleasant.

My brother Gene was in and out of hospitals in Vancouver, where doctors were trying to help him get his legs more mobile. He suffered so much with all the surgeries he had. Once, our dad packed us all in the car and we went to Children's Hospital, where he was recovering from a surgery. The doctors told us all to come, as we would probably not see him alive again.

When I was a child, I was never told that I was pretty. I thought that I must be ugly so I felt quite insecure. My mom always said that "pride comes before a fall" and that we must never be proud. I think some members of her family exhibited that very much.

One day while walking down the street to do an errand for Mom, I saw an older lady working on her flowers in the front yard. I always admired the lovely yard. She smiled at me when I walked by and said to me, "You are very pretty." I was totally taken aback and shocked.

I walked back to my home later, looked in the mirror and thought, "Maybe I am not ugly." She totally changed the way I felt and really helped my insecurity. I have always had a problem of self-image.

CHAPTER 5

Uncle Johnnie

My dad bought new cars and this is the story that my Uncle Johnnie related to my cousin's daughter Dorothy Peters about my dad.

Johnnie's Quotes

My brother-in-law (Bill) and my sister Katie moved here from Swift Current and he started his own BA Gas Station and Garage. And he says, "Johnnie, from here on you got the keys to the car."

I said, "How come?"

He said, "Because I don't know anybody around here. I don't know the streets, I don't know anybody."

Eugene Reimer was a little boy and he needed to be driven into the children's hospital in Vancouver every Saturday for treatment and he said, "If you drive Eugene on Saturday mornings to Vancouver to the hospital, you can keep the keys to the car for that night, you go wherever you want to," and he trusted me.

Joannie came with me on some of these trips (we weren't married yet) and we drove the car into Vancouver and Eugene had his treatment. We would come home and we would bring the car back to the BA Garage and he would say, "John, have you got an hour or two? Would you mind picking up Katie and taking her grocery shopping?"

I said, "Okay."

So, I'd go pick up my sister Katie, his wife, and take her grocery shopping and take it home and then he just gave me the keys to car. He'd say, "It's yours."

So, I say, "Do you mind, I'm going to pick up Joannie and go roller skating tonight?"

He says, "Go on, it's yours. You be careful. I know how you drive. You drive fast. But you be careful." I never had a wipeout with his car or a fender bender or anything except when he bought a new one. He bought a brand new Olds Cutlass. Big, big, beautiful luxury car from Salem Motors, that's where he bought it.

He said, "Oh, could you take Katie shopping again?" So I took her shopping and took her home with her groceries and I was supposed to bring the new Olds back to the garage. So, coming out of Abbotsford towards Clearbrook, I hit Gladwin Road and at the first intersection I thought, "I wonder what this baby will do," and, *pop*! Right to the floor. Speedometer was 80, 85, 90, 100, 105, and I better pull back.

Then came a long curve and the car kept accelerating and I'm on the brakes and I'm on the emergency brakes and the smoke was just everywhere. I shut off the key. I had enough brains about me at the last moment to turn off the key and the car just sat there just smoking. What happened was it was a brand-new car and brand new carpets and where the gas pedal rod went through this, the carpet bunged up in there and when I pressed on the gas pedal all the way it got hooked on the carpet and there she went. I finally got it going and took it back to the garage and he said, "What happened?" When I told him, he got on the phone and says, "Salem Motors, you can come and get your piece of sh———. You just about killed my kid brother!" (He was really his brother-in-law). Oh, he was mad! They came and got that car and he got a totally different one. He gave me anything I wanted.

The above is how I got the story, but knowing how generous my father was, I believe it.

My uncle Johnnie passed away in 2016. His wife, Joannie, now lives in a care home in Maple Ridge, BC, where my aunt Sarah is a resident as well.

CHAPTER 6

Teenage Years

S oon after my days of picking berries, I got a job in the berry plant, where I would stand beside a belt and pick off bad berries and leaves when they went over the belt. They would come to the plant from the farms on flats. Young guys would be hired to dump the berries on the belts while the girls and some ladies would work on the belts. We would work evening and night shifts. The pickers were picking the berries all day long and then the owner would take them to the plants. Later they would be shipped.

This was such a fun job and so much nicer than picking berries.

My curfew was always about eleven PM for going out as a teenager, but because we worked nights, sometimes the girls and the guys would go off to Cultus Lake to swim and cool off before going home in the early hours of the morning. We would sleep most of the day to get ready for the next day.

My parents were starting to go to a church sometimes. We became really good friends with the Townsends. Reverend Townsend was the pastor.

My best girlfriend Ruth was the pastor's daughter. Ruth and I spent many hours together and she was my best friend until after graduation when she moved away. She also became my maid of honor at my wedding. The Townsends had a son, Gordon, who also became a good friend of Murray.

During those years, my girlfriends and I had so many fun times at pajama parties at the Stewart farm on Cole Road. Because they had a large home, us girls, Ruth, Audrey and Donna Stewart, Ann Krahn, Marilyn Nelson, and I had many fun times there with pin curls in our hair and laughing lots. Audrey later on became my bridesmaid and Donna did some of the sewing for the dresses.

During the summer, I went to a youth camp in Clayburn near Abbotsford. At that camp, I really turned my life over to God.

I met a guy there when I was sixteen, who was my first serious boyfriend and who later broke my heart with a "Dear Jane" letter. In later years, I was so glad he did that. I dated other fellows, and had one serious boyfriend who later married a lovely person.

Because my dad had a garage and worked on cars, the first one in our family to get his driver's license was Ron. He fixed up an old jalopy with help from my dad at the garage. I sometimes would ride with him. I never cared about a driver's license or getting a car. The first time I even got a lesson in driving was from my boyfriend Ed later in life. I didn't like driving a car and still don't, and as later on you will hear how that I never have been the best driver in the world.

During the summers in my teen years, I met a wonderful guy, Ed Rempel, while picking strawberries on his family farm. I had a few boyfriends but no one serious then. We had dated once in a while, but he never seemed to pay much attention to me.

Myrtle-Anne & Ed – Dating

CHAPTER 7

Meeting Eddie

E ddie Rempel was with a group of guys who had the "hottest" cars in town and they would ride around them. They were so popular. Ed would wash his car every day. He polished it regularly and "lowered" it to look like a hot rod. He and his family lived on a large acreage on the corner of Huntingdon and McCallum Road.

He told me about an incident when he was a child and the family went to downtown Abbotsford which was a few miles from their farm. The whole family was having a good time and later left for home without him. He was left alone as a small child and when one of the neighbors saw him, they volunteered to take him home.

When he got home, he noticed everyone sitting around the table eating, and no one had missed him. He felt so badly about that. He commented on that later on in life, about how traumatized he was by them not noticing that he wasn't home.

He and his brothers had lots of fun on the farm. Ewald had TB of the bone, so had a disability with one of his legs. He suffered a lot with this.

Ed had a lazy eye (strabismus) and one of his eyes turned in quite significantly so he had to have many surgeries on this and on his ears for fluid building up in them. Ed had the most beautiful green eyes, which sometimes changed color depending on what color clothes he was wearing. For example, grey, blue, or azure.

I really appreciated his parents taking time for the illnesses that the family suffered. In those days, there weren't all the medical resources that the government pays for now.

Ed's parents were pacifists so when the war broke out and George, who was the oldest son, was conscripted to go, they were very upset. George later married Mary-Ellen and they moved to the USA where George became a minister. They eventually had three children, Terry, Patti-Lynn, and Darlene.

Ewald was too sick to go to war and Abe was too young. So, Abe was supposed to be in charge of hoeing the berry fields, but he liked to go down to the pool hall and play with his friends so got in lots of trouble with his dad.

Because I was on the "grad committee" when I was in grade eleven, we went to the grade twelve graduation to get ideas for our graduation.

I invited Ed to be my date for this. After that we didn't date each other, but had other friends.

I got acquainted with Ed again at the Lynden Roller Rink, where my brothers and I went roller-skating on the weekends with a lot of our friends. We would all gather in the stands with our friends. Gene would be sitting there, not skating, but we all hung around with him. He later brought a girlfriend to sit with him. He was such a popular guy. We had Cokes, French fries, and lots of fun with our group.

Ed was there with another date on one of these occasions.

He asked me to skate with him and then he skated with me all evening. I don't think his date that night, a tall blonde by the name of Mae, was impressed. We then became a steady couple. I wore his ring, which had tape all around it, to keep it from falling off.

My brothers always teased me that it was the short white shorts I wore while picking berries that he remembered and "that did it."

I did wear white shorts so that I could bleach them and wash them each night before going to the strawberry fields the next morning. They got pretty dirty each day.

He went to Phillip Sheffield High School. It later became Abbotsford Senior High, and I was in the first class graduating in 1956. Because I was on a lot of committees and the students, council, we got to choose the mascot for the school (the black panther) and the school's colors—red and black.

We had lots of fun that year. I loved school. I majored in university courses, sciences, and did some office and typing courses in my spare period.

My brother Ron dated my best friend Ruth and they went to the grad parties with Ed and I. Ron also won the BC High-school Tumbling Championship one year.

Ron went on to study electronics in university. During the summer, Ron worked as a flagman on the highways while they were working on the roads. Ron was hit by a car and was seriously injured. He missed most of a year of studies while being in Langley Memorial Hospital and other hospitals.

Ron later worked for Lenkurt Electric for many years. He traveled the world with that company spending sixteen months in the Philippian Islands. Ron later married Cecile, who was from New Brunswick and was teaching school in Vancouver. She was a French immersion teacher. Later on, she taught my grandchildren, Derek and Meredith.

I got a job with the Royal Bank and got promoted to assistant accountant. I lived at home and paid my parents twenty-five dollars per month from my $105 net salary. I bought my own bedroom furniture and had some money saved (which we later used for furniture when I got married).

Ed and I had a nice courtship, roller-skating in Lyndon, Washington, eating foot-long hotdogs in Birch Bay, and double dating with our friends. I was so in love with him, and was trying to save some money to go to nursing school in Vancouver, but we couldn't wait to be together.

About this time, my parents built a nice, bigger home in Clearbrook. The police chief who lived across the street from us cautioned my dad that the boys were driving too fast and needed to slow down.

I remember that my mom had two clotheslines out in the backyard. She had one filled with boy's pants (jeans, corduroys, etc.). The other line was shirts and undershorts, socks, etc. On other days, she washed sheets and bedding and towels.

She ironed everything, cooked wonderful meals, which were simple but nutritious. She would buy three gallons of milk a day, which my tall teenage brothers would devour. If she made hamburgers for dinner, there was one for each of us, but two for daddy, as he needed his strength for working.

Every day she would make desserts of either bread pudding or rice pudding or the most amazing custards. She made a huge pot of potatoes and some vegetables out of her garden. If the boys were still hungry, she put the peanut butter jar and bread on the table to fill up with. We went through gallons of milk, as my brothers were all in their teens and had voracious appetites.

I remember one instance when my mother had made some pies for dinner. When she went to the fridge, there was one pie missing. Murray confessed and said that he knew that he would get into trouble for eating once piece so he might as well just eat the whole thing. My mom couldn't help but smile because as a child Murray was always the one who got into trouble.

He was big for his age, and everyone expected him to behave like an older child. When asked when we were children who did something wrong, Murray would always pipe up from the time he could talk, "Murray did it." He got away with a lot with that.

My mom never allowed me to learn to cook, as she was afraid that I would "screw it up" and we couldn't afford that. I did, however, bake something each night for the lunches in the morning (either cookies or squares, etc.). I am still not a very good cook, and my boys can attest to that.

I was especially close to Roger. He was the second youngest and sort of my responsibility as mom was so busy with baby Keith.

Roger was such a sweet little guy and so cute as well as being easy to look after.

He was very athletic as were all of my brothers, so in later years he went off to Ellensburg, Washington, to study. He majored in education and went on to be a senior high principal in different districts. He married Ann and they have two wonderful kids, Bryan and Melissa. Bryan is married to Tiffany. Melissa is married to Alan, and they have two delightful boys.

When I graduated from high school, I wanted to go to nursing school or university. However, since there were no universities in Abbotsford, I asked my dad if he could help me with my education.

He said that he had six boys to help with their education and that I would just get married, so he could not help me. Later on, my brothers told me that he was not able to help them much either.

Ed wanted to go to BCIT when he had saved enough for that, but he never did go. Interestingly enough, Ed was appointed to serve on the board of governors for the BCIT much later in life by the BC government. He thoroughly enjoyed that posting and the amazing people he met, some who were also on the board.

Graduation.

CHAPTER 8

Dating Days and Marriage

So this is when we started dating in the 1954 and 1955 years.

After Ed asked me to marry him, I was very apprehensive about making this permanent decision. In those days, no one got divorced unless it was a major problem. Marriage was for life.

I did not want to make a mistake, so I went to the church and prayed about it a lot. I knew I loved him so much, and I thought about what it would be like to marry him and what he would be like when he was older.

I liked his dad a lot. He was a very intelligent man, played the piano (self-taught), read and spoke seven languages. He would get a roll of newspapers from all over the world periodically. He was a very kind and generous man. Actually, he was generous to a fault as his wife would attest to.

I thought if Ed would be like him at that age, I would surely love him.

Apparently, he was harder on the older boys when they were growing up and particularly Abe, but he mellowed later on in life when I met him.

Ed and I got engaged on Christmas Eve 1956 and got married on August 30, 1957, when he was twenty-one years old and I was nineteen.

Ed didn't have a job at the time, so he was apprehensive about asking my dad for my hand in marriage. When he did, my father asked him what he thought he would do for a living. Ed paused and replied, "I'll think of something." My father said okay. In later years, my family would all laugh at that, as he did become quite successful. I think my dad realized that Ed was a good man for me and that he would look after me well.

We went on a honeymoon to Whidbey Island, which is interesting, as we later owned a concrete and gravel business down there. It was a simple wedding with about 150 guests in the church and we used the basement for the reception.

Our honeymoon was just a long weekend, because Ed had a part-time job hauling lime for a farmer. I had some holiday time off from the bank, so I rode along with him in the dump truck. I made huge lunches to take along, as Ed was working long hours. Ed commented on how much food I brought along. I think I was used to providing for all my brothers.

We spent a lot of time with his brother Herb and his wife Verda. We went camping in the Okanagan with them after we were married. Ed did not like camping. He complained about sand in his shorts, and so camping was not his bag. Herb and Verda later had two girls, Monica and Rhonda. Monica was close to our Cheryl's age.

My brother Ron was to be our best man at our wedding. However, as I mentioned earlier, when he was working as a flagman on the highway in the summer trying to earn money for university, he was hit by a car and spent many months in the hospital in Langley.

After the wedding, I took my wedding bouquet to the hospital and saw Ron before we headed to the US border. We had a trail of friends in cars following us, so Ed told the border guys not to let them across. What fun! His brothers were anxious to follow us to our honeymoon place.

I was quite upset with my mom sometimes when I was getting married. I had very little help from her, and it seemed to me that all she cared about was Ron. I now know that was very unfair of me to feel this way.

I once asked her what I should know about marital relations. I was so very naïve. She sent me to a doctor across town and told me to ask him what I should know. She was too embarrassed to send me to our family doctor.

We were really broke when we got married. We were living on my $105 for the first few months from my net salary at the bank. Our rent was thirty-five dollars, Ed's car and ring payment was fifty dollars, and with the light bill and a bit of gas we were really stretching it. We would visit Ed's family on Saturdays and my parents on Sunday, really eating scrumptious meals. During the week, we lived on a sack of potatoes, a sack of carrots, and cracked eggs. We were too proud to ask our parents for help. I think they thought we were just nice kids who wanted to a spend time with our parents.

Ed still had his motorcycle, which he sold. He used to ride it up to my parents' place and the boys really liked it. One day he told my mom that he was going to sell it. She was really happy, but he didn't tell her that we needed the money. She just thought he was doing it to please her. We later used the funds to buy a dump truck.

Three months later Ed got a job with the truck that he had bought from his brother George (on payments) and he took off for the north. He heard that there was a job paving the Alaska Highway from Dawson Creek to Fort St. John.

Because we didn't have hardly any money, he drove up there with a tank of gas, fifty dollars, and a tent. He slept in the tent near the Peace River (fighting with the mosquitoes) until I got a transfer with the Royal Bank in Fort St. John and was able to join him three months later. I paid my parents twenty-five dollars a month to stay with them so I could save some money. It was nice to be with my brothers again.

Ed worked on the highway, hardly eating, and if he did get some money, he used it to repair the truck so it could keep working each day. He was so proud that he never missed a day of work. He got very thin.

One day his boss asked him when he had last eaten. He said that he was okay. His boss handed him twenty dollars and told him to go get some dinner. Ed bought a jar of peanut butter and some bread and spent the balance on truck parts.

Another time, the motor went on the truck and in order to get a new one, he had to pay the Priebe boys five hundred dollars to get it fixed. They worked on it all night, Ed wrote a check, and he was back to work the next day. In those days, we didn't have personal phones. Too expensive.

The problem was, I worked in the bank in Abbotsford and I didn't have that much money in my account. The manager told me I had two days to get the money in the account. We had a Ford car that my brother Murray always really liked, so I asked him if he would like to buy it for six hundred dollars. He was delighted to get this nice car. It was the car Ed had when we got married.

I started to work at the Royal Bank, when I graduated from high school and I found this job to be very helpful in my future career endeavors. The time I gained from the four years that I worked for the bank enabled me to use this experience in many other jobs. I started working on cash as a teller, was promoted to the job of "proof," and then promoted to junior accountant.

I remember using the old adding machines with numbers straight across and down. Every item added had to be entered and a handle used to pull down the entry. We had one division machine in the bank, which only a senior accountant and I were allowed to use. It was kept under lock and key. Interest was calculated by hand.

Our Wedding.

Honeymoon.

CHAPTER 9

Life in Fort St. John

So, in 1958, we started our life in Fort St. John. When I moved up there after I got my transfer, we were both working really hard. Because Ed was working such long hours, I got three jobs—as a hostess in a hotel restaurant, in the bank, and part time in a trucking company. The bank allowed me to do this if I got permission from them ahead of time as there was such a scarcity of women workers in the north. We were really doing well financially.

There were only about five hundred women to five thousand men in the boomtown of Fort St. John at the time and there were so many jobs available for women.

Ed eventually sold the truck and got a job at the Pacific Petroleum Refinery in Taylor Flats, ten 10 miles south of Fort St. John.

At first we lived in a two-room place with no running water and an "outhouse" but were really happy to be together. After a few months, we got a suite in the basement of a home, and it was nice to have running water and we could wash our dishes in the laundry sink.

We decided to buy a car and bring it up north. It was a beautiful black and yellow Ford convertible. The first thing the fellows at work asked Ed was, "Do you have a block heater in that thing?" Ed said, "What's a block heater?" We sure found out shortly.

Later on, one of the guys who worked with Ed asked if he could buy the car as he wanted to ship it to Italy to woo a girlfriend with. So, we sold the car to Sandi Mucci.

We finally moved into a two-story, two-bedroom company apartment. It was nice and now Ed and I had really good jobs. I was working full time as a bookkeeper for a large trucking company and getting paid really well.

During this period of our lives, Ed's brother, Clarence, and some of my brothers came to visit and sometimes to live with us periodically. It was interesting to experience the extreme cold.

I remember one evening, Clarence and I were walking to see a movie downtown (when Ed was on evening shift) and he said to me that my ears looked funny. I looked at his, and they did too. They were all hot and red. And I realized we both had frozen our ears. We laughed about it. The temperatures in the north could get extremely cold.

Clarence, Ed, and I had a lot of fun. One day he said to us that there was a girl in Abbotsford he really liked and wondered if he should marry her. I asked her name and he said that it was Diane Holmes. I went to school with Diane's older sister Arline, so I told him I thought they were a great family.

We were sorry to see Clarence move back to the coast but later on he asked Ed to be his best man. However, we were in the throes of my serious car accident, and I was dying, so he couldn't go to Clarence's wedding.

My brother Murray came and stayed with us sometime as he traveled in the north on one of his jobs. We had a lot of people and friends from the coast who stayed with us for a bit of time. Jobs at the coast were scarce and the north was booming.

Murray married Mary and they had two boys, Marcel and Michael. Later Murray married Ingrid and her two girls, Denise and Lori, became part of their family.

Ed and I decided not to have a child until he had a steady job at Pacific Petroleum. The day he said he had a steady job, we got pregnant and our daughter Cheryl Lynn was born nine months later on July 15, 1959. I was so excited to have a little girl, having being raised with six younger brothers. She became the light of our lives.

We had a really good life, even though I missed my family so much at the coast.

We attended the Alliance Church in Fort St John and had so many good friends. Because there were mostly young people in the north who were working at jobs there, we all became like family to each other. We would get together and play cards and rook at each other's homes and eat desserts.

One day our pastor asked Ed if he wanted to help him build a nice brick planter at the church. Ed agreed, and so one Saturday morning they arrived at the church site. Harold Thrones said to Ed, "Well, what do we do now?" Ed said that he had no idea. They both laughed as they thought the other knew what to do. So, Ed, the consummate problem solver, said, "Let's call Lux Masonry." They did the job. We got a lot of laughs out of that. Ed was always a man, who never looked at a problem but always focused on the solution to any situation that would arise in his life.

A little later, my brother Gordon and his girlfriend Diane Thomas came to live with us so that he could earn good money for his university education. Diane slept in the little room with Cheryl and Gordon slept on the couch. They stayed with us for a while, and we did some moose hunting with them. Gordon and Diane later got married in Abbotsford.

Gordon finished his education, became a high school teacher, while working and became a well-known industrial arts teacher. Because he was always looking for hardwood for his students to do their projects, he started to import hardwoods.

All the other high schools in the province heard about it. So, they started calling him for supplies. After much consideration, Diane and Gordon decided to start a hardwood business in Abbotsford.

They both worked very hard and were so frugal, working out of their basement in their home until they got established. They supplied hardwood to the high schools and later to cabinet companies.

They soon formed a company called Reimer Hardwoods, which became one of the leading hardwood companies in Canada.

Before that time, they took a year off, sold their home, and took their two children, Colin and Cathie, and traveled to various places in the world including the Orient and spent some time in New Zealand with Gordon supplementing their income by working part time and teaching in these places.

Diane and Gordon are one of the most caring, compassionate couples that I know of. With our family, our parents, and my brother Keith, they were never too busy to help when they could. There isn't anything that they would not do to help others.

We were still living in the apartment when I became pregnant with Cheryl. We had many fun times walking around the subdivision. My friend Dawn Stephenson had a daughter named Marvyl, and we are still friends to this day, even though they later moved to Calgary with the company. Dawn phoned me in December of 2015 to tell me that she was ill and dying. I was so sad about that. Marvyl phoned to tell me that she had passed away a few months later.

Cheryl Lynn was born July 15, 1959, seven pounds, two ounces in the Fort St. John hospital, after seven hours of labor. She was so beautiful, and I was "over the moon" with happiness to have a girl after having six younger brothers and no sisters.

Ed and I called her Sherry-Lynn and we were so happy. My parents came to visit and brought a beautiful metal baby carriage. They were delighted to have a first grandchild.

I could only breastfeed her for three weeks. She had colic so badly that when I would hug her, her little body would cramp up and she would cry with pain. One of my friends, who had lots of children, told me that it was probably not colic, and I think she thought it was my care of Cheryl that precipitated the cramps.

One evening, she offered to babysit and told us to go out for a few hours. We went out for dinner and had a lovely evening. When we returned, she said, "Your baby has colic." Poor little one, she had been crying all evening. She abruptly grew out of it at three months of age. She was a wonderful baby and I enjoyed motherhood so much.

On Ed's long weekends, we would drive to Abbotsford and see all his family and mine as well. My parents doted on her. My brothers carried her around like a doll.

About six months later, I kept getting phone calls from numerous companies asking me to come to work for them. Office help in Fort St. John was scarce so I could name my price for work. I finally went to work part-time at a company called Gibbs Transport where my friend Joyce Hanson worked. I did the payroll and accounts payable.

I remember doing payroll. It was not simple. One had to calculate not only hours of work, but monthly payroll for some employees. Also, some employees were paid by length of pipe or by miles traveled or by size of their trucks. Some trucks were company owned while others were driver owned. Interesting work. All calculations had to be done by hand. We didn't have computers in those days.

I had lots of ladies who offered to babysit Cheryl when Ed was on dayshift so it worked out well. I later went on to work for Kaps Transport as their office manager. I really enjoyed working. I was not afraid to tackle any challenging task.

I always enjoyed a challenge. I was excited to learn more about the business world. When I went to work for Kaps, I remember coming into the skid shed to work. These offices were normal as often they had to be moved around. All the drivers and bosses treated me with the utmost respect and I appreciated that very much.

My boss, Boomer Kap, was especially kind to me. Often he would be on the phone, and he would get up and quickly shut the door between our offices. Then he would let fly with language that I had never heard. When he was finished, he would open the door and look at me sheepishly. I pretended I never heard a thing.

Guys in the oil patch were rough and tumble men but very hardworking. The company had contracts to lay pipe all up and down the north. They worked mostly in the winter when the Muskeg was frozen.

I remember the first day that I came to work for this company. The accounts receivables and payables were stacked in big boxes under the desk totally unlooked at. Some were still in their envelopes. The two fellows working there were playing crib all day. It was quite a mess, but I loved organizing it all. There really was only enough work for one person. I really like the challenge of this kind of work.

It was very interesting working for these companies.

Ed was always a runner. He jogged many miles in Fort St. John. It was the time before running was popular. People would drive by and ask him if he wanted a ride. They couldn't understand why he would want to do that. He found it a real good stress reliever. He loved the exercise.

It is interesting that he has run all his working life. When we lived at Plateau Estates in the late 1980s, he ran the hills of Abbotsford with Byron Hall or by himself for years. He also did many biking routes and did some mini marathons and mini triathlons.

Byron calculated that in the years that they ran together at five AM before Ed would go to work, they had run the equivalent of going to middle of Mexico and back. He just confirmed this calculation with me this week. I thought it was Palm Springs, but no, he said that it was the middle of Mexico. The guys were in great shape.

It was interesting that one day, when Byron and Ed were running at five AM, it was dark outside, a bike ran into Ed and hit him in the crotch. Ed said jokingly that it almost changed his name from Ed to Edna. So, the biker said, "Why don't you run on the other side of the road?"

Ed said, "Why don't you get a light on your bike?"

Well, the next morning the guys were running on the other side of the road and wouldn't you believe it, that same biker hit Ed again. After that incident, they never saw the biker again. Ed and Byron had a lot of laughs about those incidents.

Ed was so keen on eating properly, exercising, and keeping his mind alert. Many of his family dropped dead of heart attacks. He was determined that he would avoid that in the future.

CHAPTER 10

Life in Royal Alexander Hospital (May 1960)

On May 1960, when Cheryl was just ten months old, and while Ed's mother was visiting us, we all decided to travel to Edmonton to visit Ed's sister Hertha and her husband Glenn Follis. We decided to take Ed's mother along with us. She had come up to Fort St. John from Abbotsford to visit us.

Sherry-Lynn (as we called her then) was in a bassinette in the back seat along with Ed's mother. We left at about six PM. But, as we got to the outskirts of town, Ed had a strange feeling. He felt that we should leave our baby at home with some friends who had offered to look after her.

Larry and Joyce Hanson, who were our dear friends and who didn't have any children, had offered to keep her for the weekend. I was sad that we couldn't take her to see Ed's family but Ed thought it would be too hard on Sherry-Lynn, so we turned around and took her to Hanson's home. They were delighted to have her stay with them.

Later, we found out that my mother had a huge burden about the safety of Sherry-Lynn and prayed all day for her. The burden that day left her at six thirty PM when she felt that our daughter would be safe. She had felt something awful was going to happen to her. Interesting that she hadn't prayed for me. I think God, maybe, had other plans for my life.

We continued on our way on this dark rainy evening. Ed got tired a few hours later, so I started to drive. Ed's mom was more comfortable with me driving our new Ford Fairlane, as she said that I drove slower than Ed did. It was raining really hard now, and the next thing I remember was being in the Royal Alexander Hospital in Edmonton.

Apparently, as I was driving near Whitecourt, Alberta, I came up over the hill, and a large truck hauling loading ramps from the oil fields was parked on the road beside a double line with no flares or tail lights and I crashed into the back underneath the truck.

An eyewitness (the Swamper) said that he and the driver were trying to fix a flat tire. He testified that they were beside a double white line and the taillights were out, the reflectors were dirty, and there were no flares out. It was raining really hard.

Ed's mother was catapulted to the front window from the back seat. She suffered a broken pelvis and leg and many cuts and bruises. Ed had a broken nose and shoulder injury. I apparently tried to stop the car, and had two crushed feet, internal injuries from the steering wheel, and head injuries where my head hit the header above the windshield. No one those days had seat belts in their cars. I was unconscious and had amnesia.

Ed was taken to the Mayer Thorpe Hospital but Ed's mom and I were taken by air ambulance to Edmonton.

When Ed's sister Hertha couldn't understand where we were, she started to phone the police and they found Ed in Mayer Thorpe but no sign of Ed's mom, Sherry-Lynn, or myself, so they started to phone the morgues.

The next day, they found out where we were. Ed got discharged and went to stay with his sister and family.

During my time in hospital, I nearly died many times. I was unconscious for a long time, and when I would awaken, I had tubes coming out all over my body. One day, others said they counted nine tubes attached to my body.

They stitched a nine-inch laceration in my head, operated on my abdomen, and tried to take out the ruptured bowel and blood.

They took out a large portion of my intestines. The doctor found a severed duodenum and pancreas injury. The doctor took out the bile duct and sewed me up across my abdomen. My feet were not worked on because they wanted to save my life. I was critically ill.

Because the pancreatic juices were working, they digested the stitches and I was left with a gaping hole across my whole abdomen. My parents came up from Abbotsford, and I remember asking my daddy, "Am I going to die?" My dad just started to cry, and I knew that I was in bad shape. I was in and out of consciousness for months after.

The doctors told Ed and my parents that if that wound (which was draining copious amounts of fluid) would not stop draining, I would need to go into surgery again on the Monday morning following the weekend to try and stop it. This was many weeks after I was taken to hospital. They told my family that I probably would not survive the surgery, but that I would die in this state.

My parents who were attending the Nazarene Church in Abbotsford called the church to ask for the congregation to pray for me. My friends in Fort St John were praying and Ed's family in Edmonton where Glenn was a pastor also prayed for me.

They were all specifically praying that the wound would stop draining. The nurses were changing my soaked dressings every two hours, and early Monday morning, the nurse came in and said she thought the dressing was dry.

They were amazed and when the doctor came in that morning, he cancelled the surgery.

My recovery was long and hard. I was in extreme pain and I can remember many surgeries to clean up my abdomen of abscesses and of cysts caused from the infections of ruptured bowel and blood in the abdomen. I spent the major part of the next three to four years in hospitals for surgeries for my feet and my abdomen due to the injuries I had received.

At the time of the accident, the doctors just put my feet in casts and left them crushed as it was too risky to operate on them due to my internal injuries.

I remember one incidence when I was lying in hospital, Ed's family had moved to the Calgary area, and I was so very lonely and in so much pain that I thought that I didn't want to live anymore nor fight to live. My temp went really high from the infection, and I thought if I could just see Ed, maybe I would have the will to fight to live. I had not had any visitors for such a long time, so the loneliness really got to me. I told the nurses that I just wanted to die. Just then, Ed walked into the hospital room. Wow! God knew what I needed that day. I was so happy to see him. I forged the will to try to get better again.

Our daughter Cheryl went to live with my parents and my brothers in Abbotsford for the next almost three years. They sent me pictures of her walking, her first and second birthday, and how she was being treated like a princess with my brothers and my parents carrying her around.

Lying in bed, with legs up in traction, I found the days long and unproductive. I have always had tremendous energy. I did not like being laid up, sick, and in so much pain.

After many months, a lady came by and taught me some crafts to do with my hands. I made poodle dogs out of plastic paper in various different colors. I gave them away to people who came to visit.

I remember nurses coming into my ward, along with the doctors and interns. I saw so many nurses cry when they attended me. Many thought that I was only about sixteen, as I looked young for my twenty-two years. I quoted Psalm 23 over, and over again.—especially the part of walking through the valley of death.

I was in a ward in ICU for a while with a girl who was a burn patient. She was so sick. The nurses later told me that they thought that I would die but that she would live.

Not long after that this sweet girl died, and I lived. I was shook up about that. Why was I alive and yet she died? It was sobering.

When I got pictures of Cheryl growing up at my parents' home in Abbotsford, I would just hug them, cry, and sleep with them under my pillow until they were so tear stained and rumpled that I couldn't see the images anymore.

My mom sent pictures of Cheryl's first steps, her first birthday, her riding around in my brother's car and of the third birthday. I missed her so much.

CHAPTER 11

Pain and Loneliness

My boss's private plane was coming to Edmonton and they said to Ed, "How long has it been since you have seen your wife?" When they heard it was a while, they brought him along and dropped him off at the hospital while they did their business in Edmonton. This day when Ed came, was another day, when I was really sick and lonely and wanted to die. Ed flew back with them that day.

Because we were so short on money, Ed would hitchhike to see me in Royal Alexander Hospital in Edmonton from Fort St. John. A bus trip cost fifteen dollars so he would make sure he stayed in front of a bus coming through and when it was cold, he got on the bus.

At that time, BC Medical would not pay my expenses as they said it was up to the wrongdoer to pay for it. Consequently, Ed was using up our savings and all the money he earned from his good paying job to pay hospitable bills and surgeons in Edmonton.

All along this time, we were involved in a lawsuit. When I hit the back of this truck, the driver was underneath the truck changing a tire. When I hit the truck, the driver was killed.

I remember a beautiful lady coming to visit me in the hospital and saying she was hoping I was okay. One day, I asked Ed who she was, and finally after I was a little stronger and many months later, he told me she was the widow of the man who was killed.

I was so devastated that I immediately got sicker. Ed went to the service they had for the man, but I didn't know about it at the time. They had four young children. I cried so much for this family and when I found out. It still affects me today when I think of it.

The first time I got out of the hospital for a pass, I told Ed I wanted to go to the lady's home. She agreed that we could come.

She showed me her four children lying in two bunk beds sound asleep. I was so distraught at what had happened it nearly killed me. I was very sick and walking on crutches, but the emotional pain was worse. I went back to the hospital so distraught and not knowing if I deserved to live.

Her lawyer convinced her to sue me for damages. Our lawyer convinced us to countersue the trucking company for my damages. The case took three years, went to the Supreme Court in Alberta, the appellate court in Alberta, then to the Supreme Court in Canada and then the Highest court in Canada.

I spent many days on the stand, where the lawyers questioned me on every aspect of the case, and then spent weeks questioning me on our sex life and marital relations, as I was not able to have more children due to the nature of my injuries.

Ed's father attended some of the court cases. He was particularly angry with the prosecution lawyer's questions to me and wanted to punch the lawyer. Ed had to hold him back. Sometimes I would be on the stand for weeks. It was a very trying time in my life. Enduring the pain and agony while I was on the stand with a broken body was grueling.

In every case, I was found 100 percent in the right. This is quite unusual as one is usually sometimes given a percentage of blame.

It was a very hard time in our lives. I was so sick most of that time. I went down to 102 pounds. I remember one day the top of my head was shaved from the nine-inch laceration on my head, and I noticed hair growing all over my upper lip and chin.

I asked the nurse if there was anything they could do about that and she said she would bring some "Nair" in the next day to remove the hair from my face. I guess the hormones had too many male elements in them, and that is what was happening. She also asked me if I would like to have some lipstick on, as I was so pale. "Sure," I said. "That would be nice."

I had never worn any make-up until then, as most girls my age didn't. I had naturally ruby lips, so I never bothered with it. Later that day, everyone that came to visit, doctors, nurses, and physiotherapists, all told me how much better I looked. I knew it was the lipstick, so I started to wear it all the time then.

To this date, I can remember about twenty-nine surgeries, which included the removal of fallopian tubes, ovaries, uterus, gallbladder, appendix, thyroid as well as many tumors related to infection.

Later on, I had six foot surgeries. I now have twelve screws and two plates in each foot.

Three and a half years later, I was finally awarded a sum of just over thirty thousand dollars after I paid our lawyers. Ed and I agreed to pay for this lady's costs and lawyer's fees, as she did not have any money. I felt so badly for her and her children. Presently this case would have awarded a lot more money to me, but we were just so glad to finally have it over with. In those days, large sums of money were never given in court cases.

Later on, I had surgeries on my right foot to take the joints out, use bone from the bone bank to fuse my metatarsals and tarsals along with pins and screws to try to bring my foot into alignment.

This was three years after the accident, as it was now safe for me to have this surgery. The pins and bone transplants didn't take. So, I was left with a foot that I could not walk on, and pins that lodged in the muscles and the tendons. I continued to walk with crutches with a great deal of pain.

CHAPTER 12

Reuniting with Our daughter

My parents came to our home in Fort St. John to see me during a brief period between surgeries. I said I want to keep Cheryl at home. My neighbor said she would look after her when Ed was working, and when I had to go back to hospital.

Cheryl would have nothing to do with me. I was a total stranger to her and my mom was reluctant to leave her. My dad told me that she was quite a little handful. She was really spoiled by my brothers and my parents.

I insisted that she stay and she and my parents just cried when they left. It was so hard for all of us, but I wanted her home so badly. Cheryl cried so much for my parents, as she had bonded with them. She was now three and a half and had lived with my parents since the accident when she was ten months old.

We bought a little house in the Hunter subdivision with two small bedrooms. I remember we paid $8,800 for it from Les Hunter.

There was no running water so we had a cistern under the house for water and a septic tank. Because I was so conscious of germs, we found a mouse floating in the cistern.

Poor Ed, we drained it, and Ed washed it out with bleach and we got another load from the water truck. I later learned that they had told Ed that it was not unusual as the motel in town got a cat in theirs.

My good friend next door, Jane Hunter, looked after Cheryl when I went to Edmonton for more surgeries, until Ed would get home from work.

One day when I was home from a break of surgeries, I heard on the radio that President Kennedy was shot. I told my neighbor Jane about it when she came over to see how I was. She couldn't believe it. However, we found out that this awful incident happened and Kennedy died.

Another day when I was home with Cheryl, I heard on the news that there was a horrific fire at the McMahon Plant where Ed was working. Two men were airlifted to Vancouver with severe burns and later died.

Ed, who was a supervisor at Pacific Petroleum, was sprayed with terrible chemicals. He came home, showered, and still had this awful smell about him. He was needed back at the plants so had to go back even though he was not well. We later found out that he suffered from H2S poisoning, which is hydrosulfate gas. It is a gas which Ed called "sour gas" which is something you can't smell easily as it affects your nostrils right away.

He recovered, but I often wonder if this had lasting effects on him. He was working so hard as all our money was going for doctor's bills and lawyer's bills. BC Medical would not pay my medical bills, as they said that I had to go after the wrongdoer. So, everything was in limbo. We had to go to a finance company to get some money to even get me out of the hospital on one occasion. The bank where I had worked was afraid to take a chance on giving us a loan. We were desperately poor during this time.

A few years later, a minister came to our town and asked if he could pray for me to walk again. I told him the surgeon would not operate again as the first fusions on the foot did not take. He asked me to "fast and pray" and he and the elders of the church anointed me with oil and prayed for me.

He then told me to ask the orthopedic surgeon to do another surgery and God would do the healing. When I asked the doctor to redo it again, he consented and this time he took lots of bone out of my legs to graft into the foot, put more pins in, and took all the old stuff out, took out the tarsals and metatarsals, and fused my foot. Prior to this surgery, he had used bone from the "bone bank."

God did the healing and the surgery took. I was finally able to walk without crutches after a few more months.

Cheryl Age 4.

CHAPTER 13

Cheryl and Darcy

About this time in our lives, Cheryl was growing up without any brothers or sisters. I could not have any more children. We bought a little white toy poodle named Westbrook's Mr. Magic. When Gordon and Diane were living with us, they decided to get a little female poodle and we would breed them. Well, that didn't work out well, as Mr. Magic was a snooty dog, and we had to take them to a vet to get bred. It was so funny.

A little while later, we looked after a baby boy named Darcy. His father was in a horrific plane crash and his mother was in Alberta with the father a lot. Sylvia Hole asked if would look after Darcy, as her mom had her other three children.

Ed and I became so attached to Darcy that we wanted to adopt him. Of course, his mother would not permit that. She was trying to keep her family together.

Later when his mother was home for two weeks, she asked if Darcy could be home to be with her. She missed him so much and wanted to have all her children at home with her. I am grateful for the timing of her coming home.

Darcy developed a viral pneumonia when he was at the Hole home, got very ill, and died over the weekend in the hospital. Sylvia was heartbroken.

Ed and I were devastated. Ed was his pallbearer and we both cried so much that we couldn't even go to the reception after the funeral. He was like our son. Ed and I drove for hours in the countryside that day and could hardly go home. I have not seen Ed cry many times, but this was one of them.

It was then that we knew that we could love another child as much as we loved Cheryl. Because Ed grew up in a large family of eight children and there were seven children in mine, we wanted Cheryl to have that experience too, of having fun living in a bigger family.

We moved to a larger home with running water and a nice backyard. Ed made a skating rink in the backyard for Cheryl to learn to skate and Cheryl was in some skating carnivals. I made all her clothes as I learned to sew when I was in high school.

My favorite subjects in school were art and home economics. I loved interior design and later took an interior design course at the New York School of Interior Design by correspondence. I had to go to New York to write the final exam, but that was not feasible, so I never did get my degree in Interior Design.

CHAPTER 14

Early Days with Bruce and Cheryl

After Darcy, and five years after Cheryl was born, we decided that we would apply to adopt a son. When we applied, I remember I still was walking on crutches.

God was so good. Bruce was born in the Lions Gate Hospital on January 25, 1964. We were able to fly down to get him on January 30. We were so excited to meet him. He was a wonderful baby, and grew up to be one of the most intelligent young men I knew.

It was an adoption through the Ministry of Human Resources so we have very little information on his birth parents. That does not matter because we received a letter along with his birth certificate that stated that he was our child just like he was born to us. We were so relieved when the trial period of six months was over and he was finally our child.

He and Cheryl were so cute growing up. They looked so much like brother and sister. Ed made a little skating rink out in the back-yard now for both of them.

During this time, I had to go to Edmonton for more surgeries, and I will never forget my wonderful friends, Ed and Edith Toews, who sometimes looked after Bruce while Ed was at work.

We met Ed and Edith at the Alliance Church, which we were attending at the time. Edith sometimes looked after Cheryl when I was sick also. They now live in White Rock and have become such good friends to Ed and I. Ed and my Ed loved to talk business as Ed Toews was involved in so many business enterprises, some being along with Leroy Erickson.

We also got together often with Ramona and Leroy Erickson. Both Ed Toews and Leroy were really involved in farming many sections of land in the northern area. They did very well with their enterprises but my Ed was not interested in farming.

Leroy was my doctor when he lived in Fort St. John until he went away and specialized. They moved to Dawson Creek and later we had a chance to visit them on their farm east of Dawson Creek. Ed and I also saw their most beautiful lakefront property. They use their huge estate on the lake for retreats for charity groups. They became dear friends to us.

Ed was doing so well in his job. He had just become superintendent at the McMahon Plant, and was being well paid. He liked his work and was really good at it.

Cheryl was attending the school near our home and she and the Turecki girls were active in figure skating. I made her costumes for the competitions, and she looked so cute.

Later, as I got well, I was offered so many jobs that I started working again part-time with Kaps Transport, a large trucking company, as their office manager. We built another lovely new home in Fort St. John, were active in our church, but missed our families at the coast.

We traveled down there, every opportunity that we could, but the drive was twenty hours on many unpaved roads. Ed worked shifts before he became superintendent, so we would travel down to the coast after he got off work in the morning and then get back before he started the dayshift. He would get about four days off then.

Our new home, built by Erwin Contracting, was in a lovely subdivision close to Cheryl's first grade school. It was a ranch-style house with a shaker roof (which no one in Fort St. John had) and a beautiful red door. This was unusual because of the harsh winters there.

I used to say that there were four seasons in Fort St. John—snow, mud, dust, and mosquitoes.

Ed and I had taken up golf when we arrived in Fort St. John, and because the greens were sand and we golfed mostly in the evenings before dusk, we would get eaten by bugs. When Sherry-Lynn was a baby and before my car accident, we would put her on the cart and go out at twilight if Ed was working.

Ed thought about going to BCIT and working to get a chemical engineering degree, but found out that he was making much more money than the engineers at the plant were earning.

Our life was so good. I was making huge money working and so was Ed. He had just become superintendent of the McMahon Plant. This was a job that he had worked and aspired to get for eight years.

The company had sent him to Banff School of Management in Alberta. He had finished his grade twelve education by correspondence, majoring in history and English. He loved memorizing poetry and read every history book he could get. Later on, this would be attested to the huge library he had in our home in Abbotsford.

Life in Fort St. John was good, and though we missed our families so much, we had lots of friends who were like family to us. Ed was still doing shift work until he became superintendent at the plant in Taylor. He was working only days now.

Ed's friends Ed Toews, Vern Senft, and Leroy Erickson were doing really well in farming, but Ed was never interested in that. They were buying more sections of land and expanding their portfolios.

There wasn't much entertainment in the city, but we attended all the hockey games and joined a curling league. Larry and Joyce Hanson were our close friends also. Later on, Larry got transferred with the bank and we visited them in Calgary.

One day we decided to take a trip on the Hart Highway with some friends and do a bit of camping. We had bought a homemade trailer, so we used that. Poor Cheryl, she got so bitten by "noseeums" (a type of bug) that we hurried home. Her eyes were swollen shut.

We loved our new beautiful home, and everything was great in our lives. I was feeling better, we had Cheryl and Bruce and had lots of friends.

One day, Ed heard of an Imperial Oil Bulk plant that was for sale in Langley. He talked to me and we discussed moving back to the coast. Since we had just built the home, we talked about it a lot and were undecided what to do. Life was good.

We had heard that we could put out a "fleece" to find out what was God's will for our lives. We decided that if we sold our home, that it was God's will for us to move. We talked about selling it and if it sold in six weeks, it would be His will.

Well, three days later, we had a knock on our door, from a total stranger. We did not have our home listed, nor did anyone know of our decision. The people at the door asked if we would sell our home or that if it ever went up for sale, if they could buy it. We had a price in mind and they gladly paid it and we sold our home to them.

Our friends in Fort St. John were shocked. Many of them tried to talk us out of moving, thinking our lives would really go downhill. They were just looking out for us, and I can't tell you how much they all meant to us. They were family to us. We knew how much we would miss these wonderful people whom we had grown to love so much.

My boss at Kaps Transport offered me many thousands of dollars if I would stay on for three months longer, but I told him I was needed to help Ed with his new venture.

So, after living in Fort St. John from 1958 until 1966, we packed up and moved to the coast.

Bruce.

CHAPTER 15

Leaving Fort St. John

We missed our friends a lot and they have become lifelong friendships across BC and Alberta, but we were lonesome for our families.

It was so nice to be near my parents and my brothers and their families as well as Ed's family. I could go and see my mom and dad so often.

Ed bought an Imperial Bulk Oil Plant in Langley, BC, half an hour from Abbotsford.

I did the accounting and took orders. Ed drove a truck and did the billing. Bruce was almost three years old and played in a sandbox in the yard. Cheryl was in school.

We rented a house in the Aldergrove area on some acreage, until we had enough money to build a home. There were quarter horses on the property, which we had agreed to look after for the owners. They were beautiful and since Ed had owned a horse when he was a child, he loved the experience.

We later built a nice home on half an acre in Langley.

Cheryl was seven years old and Bruce two. It took a while to build, and was on a bluff overlooking Langley on Mossey Crescent. We had a long driveway, with a grove of trees in the center. It was a beautiful home that my brother Eugene designed.

CHAPTER 16

My Dad's Accident

My dad and my brothers loved to fish. My dad owned a Royalite Oil Bulk plant. He had a white German shepherd dog that went everywhere with him in his white pickup truck.

My mom and he were finally alone. My grandmother who lived with them for a few years wanted to go into Tabor home, which she and my grandfather had established many years before. All her friends were there. My mom and dad were finally alone and having a good life at both their ages of fifty-three.

Dad loved Salmon and Cohoes fishing and went out really early before work to fish the banks of the Fraser. I bought him some hip waders for Father's Day in 1967, and he was so pleased to get them. We were still living in Langley.

I warned him about using them, as Ed knew of a fellow who drowned while fishing with them on in Fort St. John. My dad said that he knew all about safety with them and he would be careful.

One Sunday morning on June 25, 1967, at age fifty-five, when the water was really high on the Skagit River, my dad and a group of friends went up to the river there to fish. Ed's brother was there also.

The river runoff was huge from the spring rains, so as my dad was walking on the little wooden bridge, he tripped and fell in. His hip waders immediately filled up with water.

Ed's brother almost reached his hand but couldn't reach him and thankfully he didn't. Otherwise he would have been pulled in too.

The men saw Bill floating down the fast river out of sight. Not a piece of clothing or anything was ever seen again. We never found his body or anything.

It was a traumatic six months for our family. My dad's white German shepherd named Cheyenne cried and paced the shores, seemingly knowing that his master was in trouble. My brother Murray took him home, but he later had to be "put down" as he became mean and took to biting people.

I was twenty-nine years old when my dad died. My mom was devastated. My brothers called the Chilliwack Army and they searched the banks for a long time. We had helicopters looking for him, and my brothers and Ed spent many weeks searching for something or anything on the banks of the river. The Skagit drains into Ross Lake in the USA.

People at my mom's church of the Nazarene were so good to us. They told us we should have a memorial service for him. We didn't know what that was. So about six weeks or later we had one. My mom always believed that Dad would walk out from woods somewhere having had amnesia or something, but after six months we had to settle the estate.

Shortly before my father died, he gave my mother a beautiful set of china dishes. She had always had an unmatched assortment of dishes and always wanted a complete matching set. She was so thrilled when he presented this gift to her at Christmas. She treasured this set immensely. It was the most precious gift that my father had ever given her.

After my father died, and while washing these items, she broke a teacup. She was absolutely devastated and cried so much about losing this precious piece of what my dad had given her. It was her last gift from my father to her.

She mentioned to me that God had spoken to her about valuing a cup more than her relationship with her Lord. She asked God to forgive her and didn't mourn the loss any longer. In fact, she put it out of her mind, saying that material things should not be that important in her life.

About six months later, she happened to be walking through Gosling's General Store, which was a store with a variety of items for the home. As she was walking through the china department of odd items on sale, she noticed a single teacup of the exact pattern of the cup she had broken. When she asked the store manager where it came from, he told her that he had no idea. There was not another item, not a saucer or a plate, nor a cup or any other item of that pattern in the store.

Every time she went back to that department, she looked but never saw that pattern again. She told me that it was a lesson to her not to value material goods more than her walk with God. When she gave it to Him, He miraculously gave it back to her.

Years later, my brother Gordon purchased this set from the estate when it was settled. He realized how important my dad's gift to Mom was.

CHAPTER 17

Life without My Dad

My brothers and Ed and I looked after Mom, paid her bills, gave her a monthly amount to live on, and helped her through all this. She had never driven a car, paid a bill, or done any business, as my father did everything for her.

So, she had to learn how to drive and look after herself. She became quite independent, and many men wanted to date her, but she told me that no one ever measured up to Bill. We encouraged her to get out.

A funny thing happened after we fixed up the house and we built a suite downstairs, where my brother Ron stayed. She dated this one fellow, and when she got home a little after midnight, she told me that Ron said to her, "Getting home kinda late, aren't you?" She told me that she just kind of felt like she was like a delinquent child and went straight to bed. We all laughed at that. Ron was so protective of her and looked after her so well.

After the initial years following Bill's death, she went to California with us and did a few trips to Hawaii with her friends. She later sold the house and moved into James Apartments on South Fraser Way in Abbotsford. Our friends Ernie and Ardis lived there too, as did my aunt Lou when she moved to Abbotsford from Alberta after her husband died.

My mom traveled a bit after my dad died, taking a trip to Hawaii with some lady friends from the Nazarene Church. She also accompanied us to Disneyland with our children and to Tijuana, Mexico.

We had driven down to California in our white Cadillac with a black roof. An interesting thing happened to us in that one night we thought we would go to a movie, and my mom said she would be happy to stay in the hotel and look after our kids.

Well, we found a parking spot and thought we would go see the *Godfather*. When we got into the theater, which was absolutely packed, we noticed that the audience was all black people. During the movie, they were quite boisterous about the dialogue. We went back to our car, which was fine, but later learned that we were in the "infamous" Watt District.

Two years after Bill's death, she had told me one Christmas day that she had a huge lump in her breast (the size of an orange). Her doctor had given her painkillers for it.

I was appalled and I immediately got her in to see my doctor Ernie Janzen who had become our very good friend. But it was too late. Her breast cancer had now spread. She had chemo, radiation, and everything the doctors could do. Dr. Gerald Siemens became her family doctor then. He was marvelous with her.

She was able to go to Ron and Cecile's wedding in Vancouver and to Roger and Ann's wedding in Washington, but was quite sick.

She lived with Ed and I for the last three months of her life because she just wanted to get out of the hospital.

One day she said to me, "Who will pray for my boys when I am gone?"

My brother Gordon said to her, "Mom, maybe we should pray for ourselves."

We had just finished making a lovely bedroom and bathroom downstairs for Cheryl. We made a hospital bed for my mom in Cheryl's old room and nurses came and gave her morphine for pain, and other drugs. She was such a brave, uncomplaining soul and suffered so much.

One day she told me that she heard that Kathryn Kulman was in Vancouver and she said she wanted to go to the healing service. She wanted Eugene to take her as then they could both be healed.

We got a station wagon, put her in a stretcher in the back, and Eugene drove her in. She didn't want anyone else to come, but told me that today she will be healed and will be running and jumping. The service was at seven PM. I had not heard from Gene and was waiting by the phone when he finally phoned me about ten PM, and that mom had died at the meeting and he was at St. Paul's Hospital with the coroner.

He said that when she was lying at the front of the auditorium, he said to her, "Mom, Kathryn is on the platform now. Do you want to sit up?" She said yes and she died right then. I was devastated. She died on June 25, 1974, at age sixty-two. I was so angry with God. Later on, I realized that she was now healed, and was in heaven.

Cheryl and my mom were so close, and after she died, we decided to buy Cheryl a Shetland pony, which we boarded out at a farm. Her pony was called Goldie. It had a sulky cart that came with it. We hoped it would ease her pain on losing my mom. We later sold it when she went off to university. Goldie was a bit of a renegade pony, and sometimes Ed would get these calls at work saying Goldie had broken out of a fence and was on the loose. So off he would go to Aldergrove to find her.

We were now living in Abbotsford, having sold the business in Langley.

CHAPTER 18

Back to Langley and More Trauma

When we were living on the farm before we built the house on Mossey Crescent and after my dad died, we had another traumatic experience.

One late evening, I took Ed back to the plant to get his truck. We took the children out of bed and went to Langley to pick up Ed's pickup. I was in our brand new two-door Pontiac Custom sports car.

Bruce at the time had a congenital leg problem so he wore special braces on his legs at night to turn his legs out in a large angle, with special boots on his feet.

On our way, back from the plant in Langley, Ed was ahead of me in the pickup truck with Cheryl, I was in the car behind him with Bruce. It had been a really bad rainy and snowy month and there was high flooding everywhere.

It was January in 1968 and there was ice on the streets and on the water. We went over a little icy wooden bridge with wooden rails, and I braked on the bridge. I was going quite slowly but slid over the rails and ended up in the water-filled ditch, which had trees and brush covering it.

The car was upside down with only part of two of the back wheels showing above the water. As I slowly had left the road, I saw Ed's taillights disappearing in the distance. It was so black, and ice was floating on the water.

I tried the windows, but the water rushed in. I tried the horn but it didn't work. The car quickly filled up with water and I knew we were doomed.

I grabbed Bruce, held my hand over his mouth and nose, and we swam underneath the seats to find a small air pocket on the floor at the back of the car on the floorboards. I knew that I couldn't go through the floor or the trunk. It was incredibly cold with ice floating in the water.

I tried to keep Bruce from crying, because I was afraid he would use up the oxygen. I told him that we were going to be with Jesus. He said, "I don't want to go be with Jesus, I just want my daddy."

I prayed that God would accept me into heaven and asked Him to forgive me for being so caught up in my world that I wasn't making time for the important people in my life.

We were building a new home, and I was so caught up in the decor and making sure everything was right that I wasn't taking time for Him and for others. I knew I was becoming too self-absorbed and materialistic.

I prayed for forgiveness, and that I would be worthy to go to this heavenly perfect place.

It's interesting the things one thinks of when one is dying.

I worried about who would look after Ed and the office, who would do my daughter's long beautiful blonde curls, how would she be raised, and how unfair it was to Bruce to not have lived a full life.

After what seemed like a long time (but probably wasn't), I heard a noise outside.

A man and his wife were driving on this lonely dark road close to midnight. He had a large truck and so could see from up high what looked like lights in the bushes in the water. It was about midnight and he was used to looking for unusual sights, as he was a trucker from northern BC.

He said to his wife that he should back up and look again. She told him it was probably reflections of lights from houses in the distance. He said that he would take a look anyway. As he got out of his truck, he heard Bruce crying. So, he went over to side and called,

"Is anyone there?" I shouted that we were trapped. He said that he would get a tow truck, but I screamed that we didn't have time.

He left and I thought, *Oh, we are surely going to die.*

A short time later he came back. He apparently had gone to the neighbors and awoken them. He waded into the water with a crow bar. As he leaned down the air pocket disappeared and we were immersed in water.

He wrenched the door of the two-door car open. I yelled at him to take my little boy and then I swam out. We were taken to the hospital and spent the next night and day thereafter suffering from hypothermia but otherwise unhurt. Ed was finally alerted as to what had happened to us.

God had given me another chance.

CHAPTER 19

Leaving Langley

My father had died in June of 1967 and every time I went by the funeral home, I thought, *I should be in that place and my father should not have died.* This was January of 1968.

I became a very serious person and thought others were so easy-going and jovial. I can't explain how traumatized I was by this event. We finished our house in Langley and I really enjoyed living there.

In the previous car accident, I was hurt very badly, but in this one, I was not hurt at all. During this accident, I was totally aware of my plight, unlike my first accident. I had now totaled two brand new cars, each with less than ten thousand miles on them.

My uncle Johnnie told me, with a smile, that I should either get a cab or walk as I was not doing very good driving.

I remember one day, after Cheryl and Bruce were playing outside with the neighbor kids in Langley, she came running back into the house. I asked her what was wrong. And she told me that the neighbor girl did not want to play with Bruce because he was an "imposter." Cher asked her what she meant by that, and she said, "Well, he is adopted."

Cheryl retorted back to her without a beat, "My parents got to choose my brother. Your parents had to take what they got, when they got you."

I thought that was a remarkable retort from a nine-year-old. We were so proud of her.

We had a nice life in Langley but about a year later, in 1967, Ed's brother, Clarence approached him and said that he was in building homes and had an awful time getting concrete on time. Concrete trucks were never on time and were unreliable.

He mentioned that he would like to go into the concrete business. He had asked a few other guys, but when it came time to put money into the venture, they thought it was too risky. Ed said that he would like to do that, and they thought that they would like to ask their brother Ewald if he would like to join them. They also asked their other brothers, but they declined.

Ewald was in the paving business in the Williams Lake area. Ewald agreed to join them.

So the three of them decided to form a company called Rempel Bros. Concrete Ltd. They went over quite a few names, but none of them would ever consider not paying their bills, so they decided on using their own names.

Ed found a buyer for his bulk plant right away. We sold our house in Langley and moved to Abbotsford and used some of the money to put into the business. Ewald joined the brothers six months later.

The first meeting of us three couples, we confirmed the name, decided on the colors of the trucks (green, which was Ed's favorite color), and so the guys started the company in November of 1967 with a stake of eight thousand dollars each and one mixer truck. They decided to paint their trucks Wimbledon White and Lunar Green.

They made a deal with Murray and Art Blackham to go into his gravel pit, which had excellent products. They built a little lean-to on a tree to keep the rain off the phone. At first the guys were breaking bags of cement until we got the silos built.

I remember Ed saying to me one day that it would be good to have three trucks, one loading, one coming, and one going. They bought four trucks and were in business in November 1967, breaking bags of cement until we could afford a cement silo.

Ed and Clarence were driving, Ed was loading and dispatching, and Ewald was selling. They decided to go non-union. They were the only non-union company in town. They would work all hours and any days except Sundays, while union companies would only work five days a week. They decided that they would always put the customer first. Their motto was that the customer was always right. They would build their business by giving good service to their customers, and good service was their most important value.

I will come back to this story in another chapter.

CHAPTER 20

Family Histories

E d was raised in a great family. He was born in the Abbotsford hospital and lived in his family home until we got married.

His parents emigrated from Russia in 1926. Apparently, in the 1700s, his great-grandfather and the brother, who lived in Europe, decided that they wanted to scout everywhere for really good farming land.

They heard that Catherine the Great in Russia was offering people an opportunity to acquire large tracts of land to farm. They decided to travel out there and found wonderful farming areas in the Black Sea area.

Because they were pacifists, the queen said that she would honor that, and that they would not have to fight in any wars.

So the families all relocated to Russia and built a thriving farming area, hiring many local people and becoming very wealthy. They had many barns, a beautiful home and a chauffeur-driven Mercedes car.

Ed's father, Dietrich D. Rempel, married a lady named Margareta. Fast. They lived on the plantation. They had two small sons, George and Ewald.

In 1898 when D.D. Rempel was younger, the family moved to Kaukasus where he spent his childhood years and attended school. For his high school, he went to Karassan. Shortly after finishing school, he was drafted into the army and sent to the Turkish front where it was very difficult.

During the Revolution, he was drafted by the White army and served as Chauffeur at headquarters. When the Whites lost against the Communists and had to flee, he was left behind ill with typhoid. God wonderfully undertook and protected him and he eventually came home.

When the grandparents were on the farm, the grandfather was taken to prison, and the grandmother had to feed and look after soldiers. Ed's father was still in the army then. They took everything valuable out of the home. The solders forced grandmother to feed them while the family starved. Ed's grandmother wrote a wonderful book about this traumatic time in their lives. It was later translated for the family to read.

Somehow, the grandfather got back home, so they collected some valuables, which were left and what the Bolsheviks had not taken and decided to try to leave Russia.

In 1926, the last train was leaving Russia to go to Europe. D. D. and Margareta and their two boys, George and Ewald, along with some of the relatives got on this train.

I think they went via England and boarded a ship to come to Canada. The boat trip across the ocean was very treacherous and dangerous. Ed's mom suffered from severe seasickness and vowed that wherever they would land that she would never go back on the ocean. Interestingly enough, Ed suffers from seasickness as well.

Apparently, the Liberal government at the time was inviting immigrants to settle in Canada. I think this is why so many Mennonite people are grateful to the Liberal government and voted for this party for many years.

Ed's grandfather and the grandfather's brothers and all their families arrived in Manitoba. All the family came except one of the grandfather's youngest brother. He stayed in Russia, and we heard that he became agricultural minister for the Soviet government. No one has heard from him since.

All the families stayed in Manitoba for a time, but D. D. Rempel did not like the cold, so after a few years, he and his family of Margareta, George, and Ewald decided to move to the warm temperature of BC. They settled in Yarrow for a bit, and then moved to Abbotsford.

They started to build a house on a property of a few acres on the corner of McCallum and Huntingdon Road.

They lived in the basement of the house for a number of years until they could afford to finish the house. They built a two-story, and the boys slept upstairs and the girls and the parents shared the main part of the house.

The family started a strawberry farm. They had worked in Yarrow picking hops to survive. Later on they turned it into a raspberry farm and Ed's mom had a huge vegetable garden. They had many fruit trees on the farm and the boy especially liked the bing cherries.

The grandfather and D. D. didn't have much of a manual work ethic, as they had been managers of their plantation in Russia. They farmed about seven acres in berries. Times were tough for them, but they were so happy to be in a free society.

They had more children—Hertha, who left when she was seventeen to go to college and became a registered nurse, Abe, Herb, Ed, and Clarence. They also had a girl, Verna, who was the youngest. These children were all born in Abbotsford.

The Second World War came and George was conscripted into the army, which was a huge consternation to the family of pacifists. Ewald couldn't go because he had developed TB of the bone. He would suffer a lot with this disability.

Ed has so many fond memories of his life on the farm. He lived there until we got married. His oldest brother George married Mary Ellen and went into the ministry in the US. They had three children—Terry (who became a doctor), Patti-Lynn, and Darlene. They moved to the US and ministered in many cities there.

Ewald married Ethel and they have one son, Jackie.

Abe married Peggy, who had two boys, Alan and Garry. They then had three more children, Dean, Karen and Dawn.

Hertha married Glenn Follis and they went into the ministry and served in many Nazarene churches in Alberta. They had four children, Lori, Kim, Mike, and Steve.

Herb married Verda, and they have two girls, Monica and Rhonda.

Next in line was Edward, my husband.

The youngest boy was Clarence, who married Diane, and they had two children, Colleen and Gerald. Ed was closest to Herb and Clarence because they were so close in age.

Verna was the youngest and she married Mike Woloshen and has two children, Lisa and Derek. The boys always teased Verna, that she was so spoiled.

Ed's Family—spouses and parents.

Ed's Grandfather with his Sons in Russia.

CHAPTER 21

Early Youth Days

Ed and his family lived on the farm and had many good times there. They have many stories of shenanigans. Clarence used to ride his motorcycle on the Huntingdon Road standing on the seat in a daredevil pose. His parents were so aghast at so many of the stunts that the boys would do.

One day, Ed, who had just bought his first old car, was in the yard looking for the car. Ed's father, who was generous to a fault, had given the car away.

Apparently, his father's friend needed a car to go to work and didn't have one. So Mr. Rempel gave Ed's car to him, as he thought he needed it more than Ed. The man later brought it back and said that he was mad, as it had broken down.

Ed's dad gave away a lot to the needy. He would always pick up hitchhikers, and sometimes if they were going the other way, he would take them to wherever they were going.

He once picked up two men on the highway and gave them a ride to the Legion Café in Abbotsford. He later found out that they robbed the café with guns. God certainly protected this Godly man.

They sometimes went to the Mennonite church, but the boys didn't go much. Whenever Ed did go he used to visualize that some-day he would own a large fleet of trucks. He always believed in visu-alization and lived his life fulfilling his dreams.

As a child, Ed and Clarence were playing on a merry-go-round and one day, the top of the merry-go-round and hit Ed in the mouth. He lost four of his front teeth. His parents were able to get a bridge built for him in his mouth.

When Ed was about sixteen, he owned motorcycles. One was an Indian, and another one that he owned was a BSA. One day, when he was riding one of his motorcycles, a truck broadsided and hit him. The truck went through a red light. Ed was found in a ditch, the motorcycle totally demolished and Ed unconscious.

His mother was told that his head was the size of a large ball and that he would probably die, so they all rushed to hospital where he was in critical condition. His friend, who was also riding his bike with Ed, was injured as well.

Ed recovered, but he hated hospital stay, so one night when he was quite a bit better and when his brother Herb and his girlfriend Verda were visiting, he asked if he could borrow Herb's coat and go for a ride in Herb's car.

Well, Ed and his buddy snuck out of the hospital for an hour and drove around, while Herb and Verda smiled and looked into each other's eyes.

Ed and his brothers had a lot of fun at home. They were very mischievous during Halloween. I'm sure they caused their parents numerous moments of anxiety.

One day they were playing outside and got the neighbors really angry with them, so the neighbors stormed the door and told Ed's mom about them. The boys hid behind the couch as the parents sat on the sofa complaining about Herb, Clarence, and Ed. The boys later got into a lot of trouble with their parents.

Ed's parents were very lax on "dos and don'ts." They were very strict on never lying and never stealing. I really appreciated that about their family.

Ed later worked on the "cruise ships" traveling from Vancouver to Seattle. And then he worked at the local bakery for a bit. This was the only job he got fired from. His friend said to him, "Let's go for coffee." So, when they were at coffee, the boss who was at the coffee shop came in and fired them both. They were supposed to be working.

Ed was in grade eleven in Phillip Sheffield High School when he heard of a great job in Penticton, so he quit school and went to work there. His mother was very angry with him that he would do that in the last month of grade eleven. Ed's brother Herb, recalls many memories of them working in the Okanagan in very dangerous situations.

Ed & Herb's little Pipeline Adventure—(As
told to the author by Herb Rempel)

In the summer of 1953, the Trans Canada Oil Pipeline, a twenty-four-inch oil pipeline, was being constructed through the Coquihalla pass beyond Hope, BC.

Ed and Herb both needed jobs. Ed was really young, being just seventeen years of age. They each got a job commuting to the job site from their home in Abbotsford, BC. This was the time before the Coquihalla highway was built.

One drizzly morning, eighteen-year-old Herb was driving their dads blue, forty-nine Ford Sedan. They came around the curve just past the Vedder river on the old TransCanada highway.

The road was slick and they had bald tires. When Herb braked, the car slid and (if he can remember it correctly) they did a 360-degree turn ending up in a farmer's field. Herb thinks he may have hit a cow because there was blood in the field and on the cow.

Herb called Martens Motors in Yarrow and Hank Martens came out to the site and towed them out of the field. They had broken the brake lines and lost all the brake fluid.

But, being young and foolish, they decided to carry on with no brakes. They made it to Hope, BC. Beyond

Hope they had a hill to go down to the pipeline right of way. It was a one-way road so Herb commented that he hoped no other vehicle would be coming up the steep hill.

As they started down, "low and behold", a pipeline truck was coming up the road. Somehow they made it by the truck and carried on to the job site.

They worked all day and drove home that night with no brakes.

Herb still wonders to this day how they made it, and believes their personal guardian angels were working overtime that day.

They parked the car with the dented side away from the kitchen window, where their dad always sat. Their dad didn't notice the dent for a week or two. Herb doesn't remember them getting severely reprimanded from their dad. Herb commented, "good old dad."

Herb doesn't recollect when they got the brakes fixed, but thinks his dad must have had them repaired.

Later on, Ed tried to name one good thing about that forty-nine ford. The early ones were known to be "lemons". They came up with the thought that maybe the carburetor was okay.

Because, Ed and Herb, were close in age, they had a lot of fun growing up together.

Ed later completed his grade twelve in Fort. St. John and decided there that he would go into chemical engineering. However, he found out that the engineers at the gas refinery where he was working were getting paid less than he was as a supervisor. While Ed was in Fort St. John, he completed a course in Banff in the Banff School of Management.

CHAPTER 22

Building Our Life in Abbotsford

Ed and I talked about adding to our family, so when Bruce was five years old and Cheryl ten, we went to the ministry of human resources.

We asked for a child to come into our home. We were phoned in January of 1969 that a boy was born in Lionsgate Hospital in North Vancouver on December 27, 1968. We went through a vigorous interrogation because Ed was starting a business, and Human Resources weren't sure that we had the means to support another child.

January 6, 1969, Kirk William Dietrich came home to us. Before we went to the hospital, we awoke Bruce and he remembers us saying to him, "Get up, we are going to pick up your brother."

We thought it was important for him to see the hospital where he was born. It was interesting that the same nurse who had given us Bruce was now giving us Kirk. She remembered us picking up Bruce, and was so pleased to see him, and how wonderful he looked five years later.

I quit my job in Langley and stayed home for a while. I was working at Mod Industries as their accountant and interior designer for their modular homes. I loved doing that.

Kirk was an active little guy. He was so happy and smiled all the time. When he was little, he would climb out of his crib and one day when Ed got up early to go to work, he found Kirk on the dining room table.

We were so worried that he could harm himself that we finally put badminton net over his crib. He destroyed that, so we finally got a tennis net, and that worked.

One day, while I was cooking dinner, someone rang our doorbell. A gentleman had picked up Kirk. He had crawled out of the house, pulling himself up to open the latch on the front door and was found on the street. The man really chastised me. We put a hook high up on the door after so that no one could reach it easily. He spent lots of hours on the lawn in a playpen when he was a baby.

One day when Ed and I along with our boys were traveling home from a weekend in the Okanagan, we stopped at a little coffee shop near Hope, BC. Our daughter was in university.

We were sitting having lunch, laughing, and joking around. I noticed an elderly couple sitting at the next table who seemed to be watching us. As they got up to leave, they stopped by our table and commented how happy we looked as a family. They mentioned how much one boy (Bruce) looked just like his father, and the other boy (Kirk) looked like his mother. We all smiled and thanked them. We did get these comments often.

Kirk.

CHAPTER 23

Ernie and Ardis

Ardis and Ernie Janzen had just moved to Abbotsford. He had just taken a job as a general practitioner in a new doctor's office.

We met them at the Alliance church and we quickly became really good friends. Kirk was a few months old when Ardis found out she was pregnant with their first girl, Rhonda. Later, they had Seonid. We did a lot of things together, spent all our Christmas Eves together, and later joined the Sevenoaks Alliance church the same Sunday.

I had been working for Mod Industries as their accountant and interior designer for a short period of time when we sold the plant in Langley.

Ernie offered me a job in his doctor's office doing the accounting and looking after the investments of some of the doctors I worked for.

My mom and a neighbor offered to look after Kirk while I did that. Bruce and Cheryl were both in school. Ernie said that I could work my own hours and be there for my family when they got home from school. I really appreciated that.

We were not making much money when we started the company as the fellows were putting all the money back into the company to help it grow more quickly.

It was a very fun job. I loved working in a doctor's office. The doctors were so kind to me. I worked for Ernie, Gary Siemens, and later on David Lewis, Rudy Hamm, and George Wiebe. I was there for ten years. I loved medicine, and wanted to be a nurse when I graduated from high school, so this was great for me.

Ardis and Ernie and us became best friends and continued until Ernie passed away from CLL on August 31, 1998, after four years of illness. We were absolutely devastated and were with Ardis when Ernie passed away in his home at fifty-seven years of age. Rhonda and Seonid were there also.

Seonid, who was now a teacher, had married to Dereck, who was also a teacher. They were in Japan for a year teaching and got home just a short time before Ernie died. Rhonda was a surgeon and married to Aaron Davison, an ER specialist.

After Ernie died, Ed and I stayed with Ardis from early morning until late at night to answer phone calls and meet people at the door. Many people when they found out Ernie was sick wanted to visit him at home, and Ardis and I prevented them from coming in. He got his wish and died at home. He was the most popular doctor in Abbotsford and had the largest practice. We miss him still every day.

Ardis later married Norm Friesen on May 5, 2012, after being alone for many years. Norm had lost his wife, Dorothy, to cancer as well a few years before meeting Ardis.

We have great fun with Ardis and Norm. They are so happy now. They were married on a beautiful day at the outdoor Minter Gardens. It was a beautiful wedding with all their family and close friends there.

Interesting that Kirk had married Norm and Dorothy Friesen's daughter Chrystal in the late 1990s. Kirk and Chrystal were married in our home at Town Centre Tower. They later divorced. She is a lovely girl and I still keep in touch with her.

During our time in Abbotsford, while living on Woodbine Street, I got involved in doing ceramics. A lady by the name of Mrs. Funk, Ken Funk's mom, was doing a lot of ceramics in their home and workshop. She had quite a few people coming to her place to do ceramics and had a kiln that we could use to fire our work.

I spent many hours there completing projects and enjoying it so very much.

I remember a chess set that I made. It was in silver and gold. I filled the molds with buckshot to make them heavier and put felt on the bottom to make them move better. They were about six inches tall.

My brother Gordon made a beautiful table for me with squares on the top to use as a game table. The squares were made from light and dark wood. He also made a black leather top to put on the top, so that it could be used as just a plain games table. It was a very beautiful set and we spent many hours learning the game of chess.

I remember one night, Cheryl and Ed were playing for hours. They were both so competitive, that if either of them won, they had to play another game.

I also made a lot of statues for our home. One piece was of "Venus de Milo" which was done in a soft pearl color. I usually had this one in our powder room of our home.

One day, when Kirk had his friends came over to our place, one of his friends said to him, "You have a naked woman in your bathroom."

Kirk said, "Where?" When he pointed to the statue, Kirk replied, "Oh, that's just Venus de Milo."

He was so used to my work that he just dismissed it as normal.

I did a lot of other pieces, bookends and lots of other statues. Most of the pieces I have either given away or were broken.

I did a Nativity scene, which I have kept all these years and usually put out at Christmas. It is of the shepherds, wise men, and of course Mary, Joseph, and the baby Jesus. Along with these, I made camels, a donkey, sheep, a cow, and other items.

I crafted this set in soft blue, soft beige, and white colors. I have always loved the Lladro pieces, so I wanted this Nativity scene to resemble the soft colors of Lladro.

I still have it today, which my children and grandchildren enjoy. Unfortunately, most of the other pieces of ceramics are gone.

One day, when Kirk was over playing with the neighborhood boys, he called me and said to tell the boys that he was adopted and so was Bruce. I asked why and he said that they wouldn't believe him. I told him that I would, but Bruce had his own story to tell. So, on the phone comes this gruff voice asking if it was true. I said yes that it was. He growled okay.

Because, I had so many surgeries and head injuries, I had a real problem with my hair. It was very thin and very fine.

I used to get wigs especially made for me from Europe. A company in Vancouver, would take a sample of my hair from the back of my neck, and send it away to have a natural wig made for me. The wig would have big holes in it to let my natural hair be pulled through it.

It was quite costly, but it seemed that the style was always a problem.

Cheryl suggested that I take the newest one to Suki's in Vancouver to have it styled.

I took it into the shop, and Suki told me that she had a new stylist that was very good with thin hair.

She took me over to Rod, and Larry the color technician. Rod asked me if he could try something else, as he was having trouble with the wig.

I said, "of course."

So Larry, came over, and they decided to put lighter highlights over my dark hair, and cut and style it.

When Ed picked me up, he said, "Myrtle-Anne, that is the best your wig has ever looked!"

I replied that it was not a wig, but my real hair.

He said, "That's it, your going back there every day." I told him that was not practical as we lived in Abbotsford. He said, "then every other day or week." We finally agreed on either once a week or two. Now I only go back every four weeks.

I have stayed with these remarkable hairdressers for over 20 years. They have also become my friends.

25th Anniversary.

Ernie & Ardis.

CHAPTER 24

Rempel Bros. Concrete

Rempel Bros. Concrete Ltd. was formed in November of 1967. They would take orders Saturday and work into the night, while the other two companies, who were union, could not do that.

Six months later, Ewald joined them. He went out and became the salesman and looked after the banking. We now had four trucks, situated in the Blackham pit. Clarence and Ed drove the trucks and dispatched.

Our company grew very quickly, and as the guys decided it was going to be a non-union company, they could work any hours they wanted. The contractors liked that and we hired a lot of young guys. They would wash trucks and jockey trucks around the yard until they were qualified to drive. Abe, Ed's brother, became our number one driver and many of the local young men came to work for us.

Later on, my nephews Dean Rempel, Jackie Rempel, and Kevin Reimer worked for us. Dean and Kevin still work for the company.

The teamsters union was starting to take notice of us. We had now amassed over twenty trucks and had started a plant in Langley, BC. Langley was a thriving community. Ed knew of a realtor in Langley who was able to get a nice acreage for us off Glover Road. He was able to get it rezoned and we set up a new state of the art plant there.

Ed dispatched and ran the Abbotsford plant and Clarence ran the Langley plant. Our nephew, Jackie, Ewald's son, went to work out there to help him also. It was a very successful plant.

In 1975, Ed got a call that Clarence had suffered a huge heart attack at the plant at the age of thirty-five years old. Clarence had rheumatic fever when he was a child so therefore he had heart problems. He had surgery a year back on the aortic valve and was to take blood thinners, but was feeling so good after the surgery that he probably didn't take as much as what he needed.

We went to Diane and Clarence's home on June 3, 1975, after Clarence had died at the plant. It was a terrible time for all of us. As midnight rolled around on June 4 everyone wished Ed a Happy Birthday. Ed was so devastated. His best friend since childhood had just died. He cried. I had not seen Ed cry often.

We were not getting big salaries as we were putting money back into the company to help it grow. The boys asked Diane if she wanted to sell her share and she said no, so the boys paid her the same wage as they themselves were getting until she married Ernie Lobe years later. When they sold the company, Diane received the same equal share amount that Ewald and Ed received.

My working for Ernie helped our household a lot, as I still wanted my children to take swimming lessons, music lessons, enjoy skiing, etc. The boys played little league hockey. Cheryl was into cheerleading and various other activities.

During the 1970s and early 1980s, the teamsters union made a concerted effort to unionize Rempel Bros. Because we were the only non-union ready mix company, we could service all the small contractors and builders who didn't belong to a trade union. The teamsters decided that if they would unionize Rempel Bros, then therefore all the other trades would have to become union.

Our drivers were paid very well, got overtime, benefits, and were happy working for us. Many of the drivers were young guys and were not interested in joining a union and putting out union dues for a union that had a reputation for being corrupt.

We were getting lots of pressure. The cement companies Tilbury, Lafarge, and Ocean refused to sell us cement. Ed contacted a cement company in the US and they said they would sell us cement. Ed looked into railing it into Canada, but that didn't work and wasn't financially viable.

He came across a trucker, Bruce Walden, who had six cement hauling trucks and said that he was not afraid to cross picket lines in Canada and would bring it into Canada. Ed made a deal with Bruce's company, Cement Distributors Incorporated (CDI).... formerly called R-Way Leasing that rented directly to Rempel bros. Concrete to bring powder cement to our plants in Canada. It cost us a lot of money for brokerage and other costs, but we finally had cement for our concrete. Dave Walden, Bruce Walden's son mentioned to me the other day that Bruce got beat up at the Canada-U.S. border at Douglas Crossing while hauling cement into Canada. He was hurt so badly by the teamsters picketers that he could hardly walk.

About this time, other companies in BC were having major problems getting concrete and other supplies for their businesses. They kept phoning the office where Ed was general manager while Ewald was out selling and looking after the banking.

Ed saw what was happening all over the province so after talking with some businessmen, including Elmer Verigan from the interior of BC and others from Victoria to northern BC, they decided to start an association which they called ICBA (Independent Contractors and Business Association). It quickly grew all over the province as members felt they had some support to run their businesses.

Their first annual meeting was held in Abbotsford in November 1975 with Ed as president, with Ken Funk, Elmer, and Roy Moore from Victoria present. Pamela Martin was the emcee. This was just before she became a famous news announcer. We had an older gentleman who looked after the details of the office. His name was Ralph Purdy. They asked me to do the minutes. I had no experience with that, so the notes were pretty meager.

So, at this time, all over the province, Ed was fielding calls of businesses that were being strong-armed by unions. The teamsters were adamant that if the largest non-union concrete company in BC would become union, then everyone in the building trades would have to become unionized. They started using extreme scare tactics. We would see them on the running boards of our trucks and harassing our drivers. They would vandalize our trucks and our plants.

We had a new home on the corner of Ash Street and Woodbine which was just a few blocks from our Abbotsford plant.

There were carloads of big guys that would drive up and down our driveway, flashing their lights. Big men would get out of the cars, trying to intimidate our home at night. One night my mother was looking after the children when Ed and I were out to a meeting, and she was so afraid that she said she didn't want to look after the kids anymore. She said that she feared for our lives. A girlfriend that I had, said that she was afraid to go out with me, saying that if I got hurt she might get hurt also.

Our daughter Cheryl graduated from high school at fifteen. She skipped two years of school, doing grades four, five, and six in two years. She later went to Yale middle school and was being bullied badly by another girl. She decided that the only way for her to get out of that school was to study so hard that she could skip a year and go to Abbotsford Senior High School. After talking with the counselors, we decided to let her go on. She did well in school. Therefore, she had skipped two grades. At that time, we were not aware that she was being bullied.

When Cheryl was nine years old, she got rheumatic fever and was bedridden for a while at home. While she was sick, Ernie visited her often to check on her condition. One day, she and I were talking and she asked me what I thought she should do for a career.

I told her there were many options. She could be a stewardess, a nurse, a secretary, and a teacher and do many things. She asked what a nurse did. I said that they helped the doctor, took orders from him, and nursed patients. She asked what the doctor did, and I told her that he diagnosed patients and found treatment for them. So, she said, "Well, I want to be the doctor." I was a little taken aback, as not many women went into medicine in the 1960s and 1970s. She never deviated from her goal but asked me not to say anything to anyone, in case she could never complete her dreams.

One of her most embarrassing times attending Abbotsford Senior High School was when I was off to work really early and Ed was busy at work. Ed got a mixer truck and driver to drop her off at school on the driver's route to deliver concrete,

So, at sixteen, she went off to Trinity Western University for her first year. She lived at home, as she was so young and we wanted her close to home.

One day when she was driving her little Honda Civic (which we bought her for her sixteenth birthday) home from Langley, she noticed a suspicious car following her all the way from Langley, and knowing that no one was home, she drove to the Abbotsford concrete ready mix plant where her dad was. As soon as she entered the yard, the car spun away and left. We knew it was more intimidation for our family.

We were getting calls all over the province from non-union companies. Ed would send trucks to the Okanagan to haul concrete to places where they couldn't get concrete. He was working so hard, looking after our businesses, and flying in one of the member's small planes to help ICBA members.

Our first major venture was into Vancouver for a large commercial job, the Penny Farthing project and then the Sandman Inn. There was never a commercial job done by a non-union company in Vancouver. We were taking a big step. The Gaglardi family was building the Sandman Hotel non-union.

The union thought they had the Sandman Inn in their hold, and suddenly the green and white trucks rolled into town. They were livid and the picket lines were set up. One of our drivers was behind the picket lines in the job site, so Ed just jumped in a truck and drove into the site, picked up the driver, and drove out.

The air was electric and volatile to the extent that the RCMP took Ed and his nephew Jack to jail for the night to protect their lives.

Our company was in the front page of the news for months and years. This actually helped our business a lot as many small contractors sympathized with us.

We now had a reinforcing steel company, and a concrete pumper company, called Challenge Concrete Pumping.

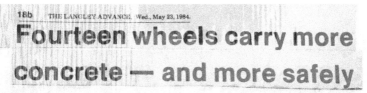

18b THE LANGLEY ADVANCE, Wed., May 23, 1984.

Fourteen wheels carry more concrete — and more safely

Western first

A first for Western Canada can be seen prowling the streets of Langley: Rempel Bros. Concrete has begun use of its first proto-type tandem steering axle mixers.

The idea was first incorporated over two years ago when Rempel began to look for a way of developing a truck and mixer with greater carrying capacity — while also increasing stability and saftey.

Because all available trucks with tandem steering axles were made in Eastern Canada or the United States and didn't meet with local requirements, Rempel found it was necessary to locally build a specifically designed unit able to transport concrete as needed.

Rempel took its problems to The Welding and Engineering Company in Vancouver and, following two years of research and development, the first proto-type model rolled off of the assembly line in January. The vehicle, a joint venture between Rempel and The Welding and Engineering Company, has the largest legal carrying capacity in Western Canada.

After its delivery to Rempel's Langley dispatch plant, the truck was put to use in all facets of the concrete business.

The unit's trial run in Langley proved highly successful and Rempel has since taken delivery of a second unit for its Abbotsford plant. The company has ordered six more units of the same design.

In addition to the increased stability and saftey over the previously used mixer or mixer-booster units, the 10.5 cubic metre

Rempel Bros. Truck.

Rempel Bros. Truck Mt. Baker.

CHAPTER 25

Expo 86

O ne day in 1984, Ed had a call from Jim Pattison, who was being paid one dollar per year by the BC government to head Expo 86. It was very exciting for the province to host this world-class event.

Jimmy asked Ed if he could come up to his office in Vancouver to talk to him. He said that the press was all over the place and that he should go two flights below his office and walk up the stairs to his floor.

Apparently (according to a *Vancouver Sun* article), Jim didn't want to go forward with building Expo. He talked to Premier Bill Bennett and said that he had a business to run. Bill said to Jimmy, "Has BC been good for you?" Jim replied that it had been very good to him.

Bill Bennett said to him, "Well, if people like you won't help because he didn't want to be tied up for the next two years, who can I go to if people like you don't help me." Pattison ended up running Expo for five years. It was under budget and on time.

Bill Bennett was a great premier, treated the public purse like it was his own, and was very frugal. He was a great builder—the Coquihalla highway (in which our concrete block company did all the medium barriers for it, along with the sea-to-sky highway), BC Place Stadium, and Sky-train.

Ed and a few guys went up to meet Jimmy, and he asked them if they could build Expo 86 non-union as the trade unions were "holding his feet to the fire."

Ed of course replied that they definitely could. We have the concrete, the steel, the contractors, the pumping company, and many trades that could finish concrete (our friend John Voth being one).

Jim said to Ed, "What about piledriving?"

Ed said no problem, that we would start a piledriving company, and in 1985, we had Griffiths Piledriving Company working and ready to do the work. As I said earlier, Ed always focused on a solution and never a problem.

Jim Pattison then went to the press and said that he would build the Expo 86 non-union unless the unions would cooperate. After many negotiations, this is the first time in BC history that union and non-union companies worked together amicably on a site. During this time, Bill and Audrey Bennett were put under full time RCMP protection during the restraint program in 1983.

The whole history of BC changed, and today there are almost even percentages of union and non-union companies working. A businessperson or contractor can have a choice. I am not saying that unions are bad, but being forced to join one, especially a corrupt one like the teamsters were back in the 1980s, is wrong. A business should have a choice and now they do.

Ed and I traveled to some ready-mix conventions in the US to get ideas and find out what is happening in the industry. After being in Houston, we decided to take a few days to go to Acapulco for a bit of relaxation.

Whenever there was a ready mix or concrete convention, we would try to go and Ed would try to pick up ideas for making the company more efficient. Ed worked six days a week and long hours so we would often take a few days after we were at a convention to visit other places near there on our way back home.

We were sitting at the pool. There were some really big guys talking loudly. One of the men had big plugs in his head for a hair transplant. Ed came over and told me that we had to leave.

We found out that the person talking rather loudly was Jimmie Hoffa's son and he was bragging about "getting those blankety-blank Rempels in Canada." This was the climate of the tensions at that time.

At one of these conventions, Ed talked to the Mack truck people about making a bigger truck so that they could haul a bigger payload. The weight laws only allowed trucks to haul an eight cubic yard load. After talking to the truck manufactures, Ed wondered if they could put extra wheels on the front of the truck and that way they could haul a bigger load. They agreed to build a bigger truck and then Ed talked to Bernie Bosher at the Welding shop, where we got all our drums made, to make the larger drums.

We got the bigger truck with the bigger concrete drum. It had wheels which went up the on the back of the truck, so that when the truck was empty it would save on the wear of the tires. We had the very first "tandem-tandem" truck in Canada.

All the other companies laughed at Rempel Bros. It is interesting that now you never see a mixer truck that is not tandem-tandem.

I just wished that Ed would have patented this truck design. He didn't care about that, he just wanted an efficient truckload to be hauled to his customers.

Later on, Jack and Ed saw a really interesting concrete batching system at one of the aggregate and concrete conventions and they implemented computerized concrete batching which was one of the first systems in BC or Western Canada.

The unit was so large that it took up a room that was ten feet by ten feet and had to have the proper humidifier and to be temperature controlled. By this time, Rempel had an office on Bourquin Road in Abbotsford where all the batching took place for all the plants. Jack was head dispatcher then.

During this time, Ed saw the opportunities in more communities other than Abbotsford, and he and Myrtle-Anne spent many hours calculating how far the mileage was from the market and where they should locate other ready-mix plants and how long it would take to get gravel there and so on. He would drive his car, and I would calculate the miles. He would pick me up at Ernie's office or at home and I would go with him often about two PM.

He used to visit each of his plants once a week. Even though he had good managers, Ed liked to visually see what was going on.

The company expanded until they had eighty-eight mixer trucks and eight plants strategically located throughout Vancouver, Abbotsford, Chilliwack, Coquitlam, Langley, and North Vancouver.

They also had portable operations at Tumbler Ridge, Trail, Port Hardy, and Hedley, BC, with over 250 employees.

As the company grew larger, Ed decided he wanted to sell it. In December 1988, Rempel Bros. Concrete Canada was sold to CBR (an international company). Ed was asked to stay on for three more years as president. During this time, he implemented a great retirement plan for his employees.

Instead of taking cash, Ed bought Rempel Bros. Concrete Inc., a concrete company in Everett, Washington and the steel company.

The steel company expanded and he and his friend Anoop Khosla became partners in Lower Mainland Steel, Lower Mainland Concrete (that supplied concrete median barriers to all the major highways in BC), and Apollo Concrete Products (which made lovely concrete paving pads, flooring, and other products). They also bought land in Delta and Abbotsford for their businesses, which they eventually sold.

Later on Ed and Dave Walden started Greenbank Sand and Gravel and Rempel Bros Concrete Inc. on Whidbey Island.

Ed working at his desk.

CHAPTER 26

Other Business Ventures

I n the 1990s, Ed and his friends Don Quast and John Voth were sitting around the pool in Palm Springs. We often took our children down there for spring break, or sometimes to Sun Valley, Idaho.

Don (who was involved in a tractor dealership) and Ed decided to start a car dealership, and Abbotsford Auto World was born.

Later they expanded and jointly formed Don Quast Hyundai. Ed and I had bought some land at the Abbotsford Auto Mall and they opened their dealership there in a brand-new building that John Voth built.

You have to be careful when you go on vacation with Ed. You might end up being in business with him.

Earlier, Ed, John, and Don were sitting around on the beach in Puerto Rico and John was looking at all the beautiful buildings and they decided to build a state of the art residential tower in Abbotsford. The partners were all tired of their big yards and houses so Town Centre Tower became a reality. The Quasts and Voths still live there.

Eugene Reimer (Myrtle-Anne's brother) became a partner in Lake Estates. Gene and Ed decided to build homes in Huntingdon, Parksville, and buying property. In Abbotsford, my brothers built a beautiful complex now called Lake Estates overlooking Mill Lake in Abbotsford.

In Parksville, Ed and Gene bought property and built five homes. Gene traveled back and forth on the ferry, and diligently stayed there until all five homes were sold and the customers were completely happy. Because of a huge downturn in the market, it took Gene five years to sell these homes.

Larry Fisher was a partner in Huntingdon Road Properties and their various ventures. We had one venture with Larry, where we had another partner who was not that reliable, and we bought a large piece of land to build a Formula One track or a golf course, but the city would not approve these ventures. So, one year later, we had to reclaim the land, and Ed spent three months from sunup to sundown supervising where our other partner had buried tree stumps, which had to be excavated and hauled away. Ed lost about ten pounds working so hard on this venture. Larry and Ed sold this piece of property and the equipment and we were so glad to get rid of it.

Ed loved playing golf and Bruce used to say that sometimes the tectonic plates of the earth are shifting as he prepares to putt.

He thinks doing the New York crosswords each day keeps his mind sharp and he loved doing them daily and completed them all.

Our life in Abbotsford on the corner of Ash and Woodbine Streets, where we built some homes that my brother Eugene designed, were nice, but then we decided to build a house at Plateau Estates. My brothers were in development there, so Ed bought a corner lot there and we built a lovely stone- and grey-colored two-story home.

This was before we decided to build Town Centre Tower.

CHAPTER 27

Family Vacations

During this time, we took some lovely holidays. One holiday was to Kauai with my brothers and their families. The children got to know each other better with their cousins. Cheryl was not with us, as she was in university.

Another holiday we took was to Waikiki with Bruce and Kirk and their cousin Gerald. We decided to go to the part of the island where there were big waves and the surfers were surfing the huge waves. This to me was totally amazing to see how talented these young guys were.

We brought along some fruit, towels and Gerald bought a fruit knife (that was very sharp to cut up the fruit) and the other goodies we had on the beach.

Near the end of the afternoon, we started to pack up our things. I put the fruit knife in one of the towels and handed it to Ed. Unfortunately, it cut through the towel, and stabbed Ed in the groin. He had huge amounts of blood coming out of his body, and we quickly went to the nearest hospital.

Unfortunately, the hospital union was striking and did not want to let anyone in. Bruce was so agitated that he went up to them and told them that they had to let us in. He and Gerald were so angry.

Later, Gerald told me that Bruce jokingly told him that it was his fault, because Gerald had brought the knife.

Finally, they let us into emergency, where the doctors told him that the wound was only a few centimeters from an artery. They suggested that Ed should have surgery the next morning. As our plane was leaving the next morning, I called Ernie Janzen, our really good friend and doctor. He said to just fly home and he would look after Ed.

Unfortunately, it took a few hours to leave the hospital as the police were there, and they were going to charge me for domestic abuse and stabbing my husband. It took a long time for us to be able to leave and with a lot of convincing on my part that I was not trying to harm Ed.

I thought they were going to take me off to jail.

All of us had to sign affidavits to say that it was an accident and not intentional. We finally got back to the hotel and left for home the next morning early.

CHAPTER 28

Woodbine Street

Cheryl was going to university and got a summer job at Rempel Bros. in their office in Langley. She met Barry Holmes there, who had a summer job as a driver there. We took our very first trip to Hawaii with Cheryl and Barry that fall.

Cheryl became engaged to Barry Holmes when she was seventeen years old and in her second year of university and they lived in the house on Woodbine Street, which we helped them get.

She and Barry had a lovely wedding in Abbotsford at the Sevenoaks church.

Ernie gave the toast to the bride, as he was our closest friend.

Barry and Cheryl had two children quite quickly and so Cheryl took two years off university but still studied at home and eventually went back to UBC. Meredith was born ten months after Derek. She was just a little over 2 pounds when she was born early.

When Cheryl went back, she commuted from Abbotsford to UBC in Vancouver by bus, transferring three times and still made it to her early classes, commuted back home and studied at night, spent time with her family and studied. I don't know how she possibly did it but it is a true test of her resilience and her determination to become a doctor.

One day, when we she was finished her MCAT and was doing interview to get into medical school, she said that her interviewer asked her what her other interests were other than medicine.

When she mentioned that she really liked sports, especially skiing and had done eight years of Toronto Conservatory Piano, he replied that he was most impressed with her diligence in piano. She didn't finish grade nine because she was now in medical school. She got in and the rest is history.

Barry was in law school and was doing his practicum with Eric Janzen and Jim Anderson in Abbotsford. He later joined their firm, and they eventually hired nannies to look after the children. Cheryl graduated and it was a wonderful event with her two children, Barry, and our boys, which we all attended in June 1985.

As our gift to the family, we decided to go on a "bare boat cruise" in the British Virgin Islands. We chartered a forty-seven-foot Maple Leaf sailboat and it was one of the best ten-day holidays our family had ever been on. Barry had great sailing experience and Ed had taken some courses as well.

On one of our family holidays in Maui, our family had all taken scuba diving courses, so the boys and Ed and us all scuba dived in the beautiful Caribbean waters. I remember, fearless Kirk would dive off the mast of the boat into the water and often he would find treasures on the ocean floor. The boys found a shipwreck that they went through and Kirk once came up with a US dollar bill.

Our favorite island was Sandy Cay. It had absolutely the most beautiful white sands around the grove of trees. Later on, Ed and I were trying to think of a name for our family holding company, and Ed came up with the name Sandy Key Investments Ltd. (SKI for short, as we all loved skiing). Well, I wasn't so good at skiing as I had bad feet.

Later on, we had Sandy Key Investments (US) Ltd. (for our US companies), Sandy Key Auto Ltd. (for our auto dealership), Sandy Key Developments Ltd. (for our land purchases), and a few other companies.

As the boys were growing up on Ash and Woodbine Street, they both worked at the gravel pit washing trucks from the time they were about thirteen to fourteen years of age after school and Saturdays.

My brother Murray and his then-wife Mary built a home down the street from us. Their boys Michael and Marcel had lots of fun playing with Kirk.

We all worked hard. Bruce was sweeping out the shop one day. Ed had promised him two dollars for sweeping it out one afternoon after school. I think he was about nine years old. There was a truck in the shop, so he just swept around it, and when he asked Ed for the money, Ed said they had to move the truck and Bruce would have to sweep that too. Bruce said that wasn't part of the contract. We all got a kick out of that, but Ed made him do it anyway.

Later, the boys spent many hours playing "road hockey" with the neighborhood boys and later were very active in minor hockey in town. Because there was only one arena in town, parents had to get up really early to take them to the arena. Ed would take them to the arena and I would pick them up later to get ready for school before I went to work.

Starting out, Ed worked six days a week and very long hours. He was so exhausted when he got home that our only time was dinnertime when we all had dinner together before the boys were old enough to wash trucks.

We had great conversations then with our little family until Cher went off to university. Cheryl was really young in grade twelve, and I remember one day there was three guys in our home wanting to date her. One was in the family room, one was in the living room, and then the doorbell rang and there was Barry Holmes. It was quite funny to look back on.

Cheryl had met Barry the summer she went off to university. She was working at the Langley plant doing filing and Barry was supplementing his income while he was going to law school by driving a mixer truck in Langley. They later started dating while he met her at the plant.

Cheryl was going to university and got a summer job at Rempel Bros.

As I wrote earlier, I remember when little James Derek Holmes was born. He was so cute and I was so proud of him, I could hardly keep my hands off him. He became very close to his grandfather Oliver Holmes, as Oliver was such an outdoorsman and camper, etc.

Ed was too busy working and didn't have those handyman skills.

When Meredith came along at just over two pounds, it was such a miracle that she lived. She spent three months in Vancouver Hospital. Cheryl would take breastmilk into the hospital in Vancouver and asked the nurses to save it to feed her. Meredith survived many challenges and so when Cheryl and Barry would be away, I would look after her and Derek would often go to the Holmes home.

I enjoyed these times so much, as I had missed these years with Cheryl, and now I had another little girl around to dress, spoil, and play with.

During this time, I was working for Ernie. When the boys were working, I was doing all the yard work, all the housework, meals, and laundry, taking some university courses and drawing and painting a bit.

The worst part of my life was enduring all the pain in my feet, particularly my right foot. I walked with pain for a number of years until I finally had four more surgeries on both feet.

The good news is that I can walk pain free now, although both my feet are fused and cannot move other than my ankles. They are both numb also.

Also, the biggest problem for me was my migraine headaches. I started having them when I had my ovaries removed after my first accident. I had experienced menopause at twenty three years of age.

Because I didn't have ovaries the doctors prescribed hormones. In those days, they were not really perfected. I suffered for years with migraines. I would have them for three days, and then maybe have three to five days off and then have them again.

The doctors I worked for tried everything to alleviate my pain. I spent lots of evenings in emergency. They tried Demerol, morphine, oxygen therapy, but nothing would work. Often, they would come on during the night. I think they were called cluster headaches. Dr. George Wiebe especially recommended different treatments for me.

So, I just lived with them. The narcotics made me sick, so I didn't want to take them. I remember doing some paintings while suffering at night with the pain and tried to get my mind off the pain. Our son Kirk told me that some of the best paintings I had done in the early days were when I had a migraine. Crazy.

Later on, when we moved to Plateau Estates, I remember one day Ed was watching TV and he said, 'Myrtle-Anne, listen to this. There is a new drug out that is a real help to migraine sufferers. It was called Imitrex." We phoned our friend Ernie Janzen and he said that we should try it.

Well, he prescribed it for me, I tried it, and it totally changed my life.

If I feel a migraine coming on, or even if I am in the throes of one, if I take one pill, it totally aborts the headache.

I can't begin to tell you how wonderfully this drug has helped me. It was very expensive, ten dollars per pill, but I only need one. To this day, I keep this pill in my purse, night table, and in my luggage.

Thankfully, as I have gotten older, I don't need it as often. I find that the change in the barometric pressure has a lot to do with it.

When we were living on Woodbine Street, we decided to build a house on the extra lot we had next door. Cheryl had just married Barry and he wanted to live on Woodbine Street, so we traded Barry for some property he had, and gave the house to them.

We had bought two lots side by side which we had landscaped all the extra space. We thought that it was a waste of property so we had Eugene design a nice big two-story house.

It was a beautiful two-story home with a finished basement. We built it in a Tudor-style home in shades of grey and with granite stone facing. On the inside, we had three fireplaces with one in the bedroom. The boys each had their own bedroom with a loft across from the bedrooms for their use for entertainment.

We only lived in this home for two years, as my brothers were developing a subdivision at Plateau Estates.

We had also bought a lot on Glenn Mountain with a gorgeous view of the valley and Mount Baker. We bought it for the future, intending to build on it someday.

Ed had talked to my brothers who were developing Plateau Estates. They talked Ed into buying a lot there. Initially, I was not in favor of building on Plateau Estates, but then I agreed.

Gordon, Murray, Myrtle-Anne, Ron and Roger,
after the passing of Keith and Eugene.

CHAPTER 29

Plateau Estates

I had a lot of fun decorating the house on Ash Street, but when Ed said that he wanted to build on Plateau Estates, we got the best lot and Eugene designed a house which was a mirror image of the one we had on Ash Street with a few changes. We had a good life with the boys there.

My brothers Ron and Murray both built houses in that subdivision. The property had twenty-five homes on it and a lovely indoor-outdoor swimming pool on it. There were also two beautiful lighted tennis courts. They were state of the art facilities.

Ed and I would play tennis every week with some friends and would often play doubles matches. I have never been very good at sports and am not at all competitive. I remember one evening; we were playing doubles with another couple and I kept looking at the hedges from our place and thinking that they probably needed trimming as the ball went past me. Ed asked me what I was thinking about and when I told him, he said, "Myrtle-Anne, concentrate!" Poor Ed, I was not a good partner.

Bruce was so athletic, and had such good hand-eye coordination that he was really good in all sports. He excelled in hockey, played on the "rep team," and was terrific at tennis. Byron Hall tells me that he always enjoyed playing tennis with Bruce.

Bruce kept saying to me that I had to keep moving when the ball was coming to me. I always tell people that I am a good armchair athlete. I love watching sports on TV but don't like to compete.

When we moved to Plateau, our dog, Duffels came up there also.

We had previously had him for quite a few years. He was an interesting dog. He would let thieves into our home on Ash Street, but would bite my aunt Lou. He used to lie on a bit of a dip in the pavement in the middle of one of the busiest streets in town. The cars going by would always screech to avoid him. Well, one day a car hit him, and he suffered a broken leg.

When Ed took him to the vet, the vet asked Ed what he wanted to do about his leg. Ed asked him, "What do you normally do with a dog with a broken leg?" The vet replied that they normally put it in a cast. We think he was implying that the dog wasn't worth the money of the cast. Well, we got a cast put on and wouldn't you know, after a few days, Duffels chewed the cast off, and we had to replace it four times. We finally had a muzzle put on his face to keep him from chewing it off.

The boys became really close to this dog, as he was the only pet we ever had. When we moved to Plateau, he was getting old and quite incontinent. He seemed to be very disorientated in his new surroundings and made a few messes on the white carpet in the living room.

Ed was so good at cleaning them up, but one day, he had enough, and told me he was taking the dog to the vet to be put down. It was the middle of the day and they boys were at school.

Ed came home, and I said to him that I was surprised that he did it. Ed was such a softy. He told me that he should not have done it so he phoned the vet to stop it. But the vet had already put him to sleep.

That night, when we had dinner, the boys kept looking for Duffels, and finally just before they went to sleep, they asked us where he was.

Finally, Ed had to tell them what had happened. Bruce was so upset that he asked, "How could you possibly do that? When you get old and incontinent, should I put you down?"

It took him a long time for him to forgive us, but later in life, he felt better, knowing that Ed had tried to stop it.

Kirk always had a hard time in school as he is ADD and has dyslexia. Coming to Clearbrook Elementary School was really good for him. He is very artistic. When he was doing homework on the dining room table, I often saw him drawing pictures in his notebooks (not much homework was getting done sometimes).

A teacher at Clearbrook Elementary School really helped him and took an interest in him. He succeeded in passing his grades well in this school. We later put him into MEI school for one year but he didn't like it, so he then attended Mowatt School and did much better there.

Bruce had graduated from Abbotsford Senior High, as had Cheryl.

Bruce eventually moved out to a condo that he had bought in a development that my brothers built called Alameda Court. He was still working at Rempel Bros., but did some business on the side and did really well. He also went into the nightclub business with a friend and sold it at a profit.

One day Kirk talked to Ed and I about a boy named Blake Timmerman that was at his school and had nowhere to live, as his parents were not in his life.

He asked us if Blake could stay in our basement for a little while. We thought about it and met Blake. He was a tall, very skinny, good-looking boy with long curly hair. We told him that he could stay with us, but that we had certain rules.

No drugs, no alcohol, and we wanted to know what time he was to be home at night, as I would worry about him.

He agreed to that, and was very grateful when we allowed him to have Bruce's room. He was a model kid when he lived with us. We were very lucky, and he lived with us for about a year. Ed gave him a job washing trucks at night, and I always brought the boys dinner down to the plant.

Blake had a guitar and played and composed music in that room. Sometimes he would play classical music and Ed and I would comment on it. He told us that he played it especially for us.

One day, when I was cleaning up the bathroom between Kirk and Blake's room, I noticed an essay lying on the counter.

It was titled "The people who have made a difference in my life." I read it and it talked about how Ed and I had done so much for him and how grateful he was to live with us.

I was so touched and told him when he got home that I had read it and hadn't meant to snoop, but he said that he had left it there intentionally for me to read. It made me want to cry.

He graduated that year, and Ed told him he could have a job as long as he liked and he would train him in the business, but he told Ed a little while longer that he really wanted to pursue his music. He was a very talented young man. He came to our home at Christmas time to leave us cards, but we didn't keep in touch with him.

Kirk mentioned to me lately that he had married to one of the principal's daughters and has some children now. I am so happy for Blake.

When we were living at Plateau Estates, Emily Voth, my good friend and neighbor across the street, used to tease me about throwing the Christmas lights on our trees from the balcony in our bedroom. Also, she would see me trying to kill the moles on our beautiful lawn wearing my fur coat in the early morning hours. One day, I nearly gassed myself as I put the canisters down the holes and some delayed coming off. We chuckled about that.

If I would miss the garbage truck coming up the mountain, I would run out and put my garbage out beside hers as our house was first and hers was last for pickup.

Emily and John Voth and Ed and I have been neighbors for at least thirty-five years, both at Plateau Estates and Town Centre Tower. We are the best of friends.

Ed always liked a cool room when he slept so he would keep the French doors open in the bedroom at night. One morning he awoke to find me wearing a Rempel Bros. baseball hat on my head to keep warm. He got a real kick out of that.

We had many good times during these years in this beautiful subdivision. Many of our neighbors are still our good friends. We lived at Plateau Estates for eleven years.

By now Bruce was on his own working on jobs for the company in Vancouver, the Hedley mine, and managing a part of the new sky train bridge across the Fraser River. He also worked on a few other sites. He was always a good businessman.

Later on he married Melody in Maui with only a few family members there. It was a beautiful wedding on the point of the Four Seasons Hotel property in 1990, but they separated in 2002. They have two girls, Samantha Dawn and Alyssa Ann.

During the years that we lived in Abbotsford, I was very busy. Ed was working long hours, six days a week. The boys were working at the plant washing trucks and doing miscellaneous jobs, after school and on Saturdays. Cheryl was away in university.

I was doing my university courses, working full time and engaging in all my art activities as well as church and civic activities. I was ferrying the boys to school activities, hockey practice, swimming lessons, piano lessons and all the other events that they were involved in.

Because, I was also doing all the work on our half an acre of landscaped lot, as well as cooking, cleaning, laundry and buying groceries, I was really tired.

I have always had lots of energy, but Ed and I decided that I should quit my full-time job in the office. I was so used to being very busy and making every minute count. I used to think that if I couldn't get everything done in the daytime, there was always the night.

I remember thinking when I was out with my friend Mikki, or with another friend Gloria, that they were so relaxed. They would meet someone on the street and stop to chat for as long as they liked. I was not like that and envied them in a way. I always had to get to the next meeting or errand, or be busy doing some other task. I only took time for brief encounters with people.

When I quit work, it was like this huge vacuum was in my life. I would go to a certain event, and think, "Why are they taking so long to say something for half an hour which could be said in fifteen minutes". I was so used to this treadmill of activity that I was on, where every minute counted, that I couldn't enjoy the simple things in life. I was so scheduled.

It took me about six months to gradually get over not feeling guilty. It is interesting that the guilt for not being busy, stayed with me, for that amount of time. Finally, I could relax more, with empty places in my schedule and take more time with people. I am still pretty active, but I enjoy times when I can relax, visit friends and family, and reflect on important things in my life.

I must say however, that I have always enjoyed working.

CHAPTER 30

Kirk

After Bruce left home, Ed and I spent many good times with Kirk up on the ski hills and traveling around to dirt bike tracks.

Kirk was a bit of a daredevil. He wouldn't turn on the ski hills, but would go straight down, boom, boom, over moguls, etc.

He and Ed spent many Saturdays when Ed was not working going to various places in BC skiing. Often, they would go to Mount Baker in Washington. Kirk says that he has fond memories of those times. He and Ed would have good talks during their lunchtimes.

He loved racing on dirt bike tracks and won many medals all over BC. Ed and I would load up the pickup truck and travel all over the province for competitions. Sometimes we would take a friend of his with us. One time he broke his collarbone and a few other times he would be injured.

He always warned me not to make a noise cheering for him or to run out on the track if he was injured. At one meet, he was leading, but while going over a really steep track, the chain from his bike came off and he had a really bad tumble. The people in the stands were frightened that he was hurt but he just got right back up and kicked the bike. So, we knew he was okay. I didn't dare leave my seat.

I often wonder if Kirk didn't get his sore knees from either the skiing or the motorcycle jumping.

Kirk has always been what I call my joy child. He is so funny and always makes me laugh. He is always there for me, at the drop of a hat, and helps me so much whenever I ask him to. He certainly has his challenges even now. Kirk is so generous with his time and talents, and is a very hard-working man. He loves his job, and I am so proud of him.

Kirk married Lori Hampton when he was quite young and I am so glad he did, because they had Shae-Lynn two years later. Right after they had her, he developed cancer and couldn't have any more children. It was a blessing that he had one child. Shae-Lynn is now with Evyn Bartlett and they have two lovely little girls, Sydney and Elyse.

Kirk went to Waikiki in January of 2002 where he got a job in the construction industry. He was always very handy with his hands. Ed and I went over to see him there. It was good to see him. Ed had shipped his motorcycle out there for him to enjoy.

He really liked working and living there. He only came back to BC because he missed his daughter Shae-Lynn so much. Kirk had a real encounter spiritually with God when he was living there.

He later on worked in Greenback at our Rempel Bros. Concrete operation. He was there for a few years. He now works in the construction industry in the Fraser Valley and Vancouver. His time in the gravel pit is where he learned to operate all kinds of machinery including backhoes, excavators, and many other pieces of machinery. He also learned to drive a truck and has his class one license. He has also kept up his first aid training.

Interesting, that a few years ago, he found his birthmother. He phoned me one day and asked me to have lunch with him. He told me apprehensively that he had spoken and met his birth mother. I was so happy that he has connected with her. The first thing that he told me was that she asked him if he had a good life. He told her that he had won the lottery when he got us as parents. I am so glad that he has connected with her. She is nice and Kirk has a half-brother, which is nice for him. She is only fifteen years older than Kirk. She was really young when she got pregnant. He knows who his birth father is, but has not connected with him. One day he asked me for some baby and childhood pictures of himself that he could give his birthmother for her birthday. So, I photocopied quite a few photos. Kirk does see her quite often, and I am so happy about that.

Letter from Kirk.

Kirk's Daughter Shae-Lynn, and her girls - Sydney & Elyse

CHAPTER 31

Rempel Bros. Sale

During the time we lived at Plateau Estates, we became estranged from our daughter and her husband. We were not able to see our grandchildren for two years. We were brokenhearted. This was in no way Cheryl's fault and she was not aware of the problem.

A lot of it was due to the fact that we had Rempel Brothers, so in 1988, Ed told me that it was not worth having the company if we couldn't have our daughter in our lives.

A cement company from the USA had a right of first refusal on our company. Ed went down to Los Angeles to talk to the management of that company.

They were thrilled and came to Canada to look over the company. It was a thriving business. After a period of long negotiation, we sold the company in December of 1988. Ed agreed to stay on as president of the company for three years, and Bruce had a contract to stay on for a year. During this time, Ed put in some really good pension plans for the employees.

We had eighty-eight mixer trucks, concrete pumping trucks, a steel company, and a piledriving company along with eight plants all over the valley and Vancouver. The buyers were connected with CBR, a European company, associated with Lehigh. They only wanted the concrete plants and Rempel Bros. Concrete in Canada.

So, to make the deal work, Ewald and Jack decided to take Griffiths Piledriving. We sold Challenge Concrete Pumping to the manager of it. Ed agreed to take Rempel Bros. Concrete in the USA, which was located in Everett, Washington. We later bought 186 acres of property on Whidbey Island and expanded to have a concrete operation there. Later on Ed also started Lower Mainland Steel and Apollo Concrete products with some partners.

The company was sold with Diane (Clarence's widow) getting all cash and the rest divided equally between the partners. Diane's company was called Daytona. Ewald's company was called Jenner Opey. Our company Sandy Key Investments held our family shares.

All three of us got an equal share proportionately.

Many accountants and lawyers did the division of the assets of the company. They devised an equal share plan for the three partners.

We kind of got the short end of the deal, as we had to take most of the small companies to make it work and didn't get much cash.

However, we were just happy to be finally at peace about the deal.

Unfortunately, it didn't help with the estrangement with our daughter for a few years.

I used to go to the school where Meredith and Derek attended and stand by the fence hoping to get a glimpse of them. Christmas was awful for us. I know that Cheryl was hurting very much too, but kept herself immersed in her studies.

CHAPTER 32

Trip to Kenya

The Christmas of 1986, our partner in the steel company, Anoop Khosla, approached Ed about us going to Kenya with him and Aneera. His family was from there and he was going to see them for three weeks.

We didn't want to stay home for Christmas, so Bruce, Kirk, and I joined the Khoslas and traveled to Kenya. At first, I didn't want to go and told Ed and Bruce and Kirk that I would go to Palm Springs instead, but Bruce was adamant that I should go also.

It turned out to be a wonderful trip. The first day upon arriving in Nairobi, we stayed in a nice hotel. We had a street view room and the boys had a back room overlooking a big garbage dump. When I asked the boys in the morning how they were, Bruce said to me, "Look outside, Mom, see that dump," and I said they must have cleaned it up as most of it was gone.

Bruce had tears in his eyes and said that all night people were scavenging in the dump taking things out of it.

The Khosla family was so good to us. They arranged everything for us. We went on a safari, met their family, and they just looked after us so well. They even took us to the Mount Kenya Safari Club on the equator for a few days.

It was so beautiful that I sketched a lot of ideas, and eventually did a few paintings from this trip, which I eventually sold.

I think this trip totally changed our boys' lives as they realized how fortunate they were to live in a wonderful country called Canada. The poverty in Kenya was so evident and so many people just wanted money to send their kids to school. While we were in Kenya, we bought some really lovely soapstone carvings and had them shipped home. Bruce and Kirk also bought lovely Tanzanian and garnet stones which were found locally.

After Nairobi, we went to Mombasa Beach and spent a week there. Bruce was always so generous and as soon as we arrived on the beach there, he gave a boy looking after him a tip of twenty dollars. This young guy would watch Bruce's every move and would give him anything he wanted. I think this was the most money he had ever seen.

It was a lovely restful time and then we went off to Amsterdam and London for the final leg home.

We had a lovely time in London, went up to see Stonehenge, and toured all over London. Anoop and Neera were so gracious. While we were in London, I finally persuaded the boys to go to a live theatre show with us. They were hesitant at first, but we saw a play called "Run for your Wife", which was one of the funniest comedies that we had ever seen. Bruce, then got hooked on live theatre, and enjoyed many plays later on in his life.

After living at Plateau Estates for eleven years, Ed and I were finally on our own and decided to sell our home when Ed's contract with Rempel Bros. was up.

We rented an apartment in Vancouver at 1010 Beach Avenue. We absolutely loved it, so after a few years, we decided to buy in 1012 Beach Avenue of 1,750 square feet on the water of False Creek.

I absolutely loved it. I would stand on the patio and weep at the beautiful sights and the smell of salt air. I would see the fog roll in over the water with the buildings shining over the fog. I loved Vancouver. Ed and I had some wonderful years there.

During some of these years, Ed worked in the US in Greenbank where we still had the share of Rempel Bros. Inc. Kirk and Gerald also worked alongside Ed. Later on, our grandson Derek worked there also. All the boys learned a lot about gravel operation.

Cheryl

About this time, we reconnected with our daughter and grandchildren. It was wonderful and Ed and I were so happy to have them in our lives again.

I remember a time, years earlier when we went skiing in Sun Valley, Idaho, during spring break. Cheryl just loved skiing. We all had a wonderful time. The boys and Ed and Cheryl skied every mountain. It was the spring of Cheryl's last year of high school. She was only fifteen years of age.

As we were driving home in our Blazer SUV, she said, "Mom and Dad, I have something to talk to you about. I have decided not to go to university. I like skiing so much, that I am going pursue skiing as a career."

Ed and I looked at each other and didn't say anything, but about a month later, she was back looking forward to university. She is still an avid skier and loves doing all sports, just like her dad.

When Cheryl graduated from medical school in June of 1985, she completed her internship at Royal Columbian Hospital. She started a general practice in Abbotsford and was there for ten years. She and some other partners built a lovely clinic on Simon Avenue and she was an investor in this building for many years.

After her children were off to university, she and Barry bought a boat, which they lived on for a few years.

The amazing thing about our daughter was that she never stopped wanting to learn and so she wanted to go on to specialize. I am somewhat like her in that I have a "thirst for learning."

All the time she was writing her Canadian degrees, she was writing her American boards as well so that she would have the option to practice in the USA.

She and Barry built a beautiful home in Glenn Mountain on a lot that we owned. They later sold this home and decided to buy a fifty-three-foot boat and live in Vancouver. They divorced after twenty-six years of marriage.

Cheryl started her career again with a degree in internal medicine and in critical care medicine which she worked on from 1995 to 2000.

During this time, Cheryl, Ed, and I became really close again, and she wanted to make up for all the years we were estranged from her. It was so great to have her in our lives again.

Cheryl moved to Kelowna and was in charge of intensive care for the Kelowna Hospital and for a time directed patients all over the province.

Dr. Holmes joined the Southern Medical Program (SMP) in 2009 as site director, Kelowna. Over seven years she developed it for the UBC Okanagan medical students. She received the Canadian Association for Medical Education (CAM) certificate of merit award.

Her passion for medical education and assessment motivated her to pursue a master's degree in Health Professions Education in Chicago, Illinois, in 2010 to 2014.

Her thesis, entitled "Harnessing the Hidden Curriculum in Clinic Clerkship: A Four-Step Reflective Competency Approach," was selected by the master's program for "Best Thesis" award and has been published in a peer review journal. As I am writing this, Cheryl has been chosen as Assistant Dean of Curriculum for UBC. I am so excited for her in this new field of medicine. She is Clinical Associate Professor in the Department of Medicine in UBC.

Cheryl married Denis Lampron in a beautiful ceremony in her home overlooking the Okanagan Lake on July 15, 2012. It was a gorgeous day with close family and friends there. They are very happy.

Ed and I were so proud of her accomplishments. She worked so very hard, and wrote many papers, which were published in medical journals, including the *New England Journal of Medicine* (which many consider the "bible of medicine").

Denis and I were able to accompany Cheryl when she received her awards in Chicago. We stayed at the Trump Hotel and had a wonderful few days there. I was able to tour some of the wonderful museums and art galleries there.

Some of my favorite modern artists were showing their works of art there including my favorite glass blower, David Chuily.

One of the very fun things that Cheryl did for Ed and me was to go to Wigwam Inn near Vancouver. It was a lovely weekend, so Cheryl hired a Float Plane from Coal Harbor and we flew over to the Royal Vancouver Yacht Club Outstation at Wigwam Inn. All the club members were there with their boats including Derek and Victoria on their boat *Cavocay*. We spent the day there and the three of us flew back to Coal Harbor at the end of the day. It was so relaxing. Cheryl, Ed, and I are members of the club.

Derek was in university in Victoria and Meredith was in university in Simon Fraser. Derek decided that he didn't want to go into medicine but got a degree in science in environmental studies, which helped him in his career later on in life. When he worked some summers at our gravel pit on Whidbey Island with Bruce and they became good friends.

Later on, he went into business with his father in the gravel business.

After a time period, he got a great job with Burnco and manages their gravel operations in BC. He married Victoria in Las Vegas. They had a beautiful wedding at the Venetian Hotel, with the reception at the top of the Stratosphere. Cheryl, Barry, and Meredith were all there, as well as Ed and I. Victoria's two boys, Chase and Spence, were also there, as well as the close friends of Derek and Victoria.

A year later, Derek and Victoria had a son named Oliver. He is a little Derek and I often mistakenly call him Derek. He is so much like his father—mischievous but very bright.

Meredith completed her law degree in Moncton in a totally French university, studying English law. We were so proud of this little preemie baby who got called to the bar. She later married Tony Domina and they have two girls, Richardina and Vanessa. At this writing, she is practicing in Ottawa and Tony is teaching at the University of Ottawa. They are relocating in Abbotsford.

We are all so excited to have them back at the coast so we can spend more time with them. Cheryl is especially happy to have them come to BC. The girls have spent many summers enjoying Cheryl's pool and the activities in Kelowna.

Cheryl's Professinal Photo.

*Cheryl's son Derek with his wife Victoria and
their sons, Chase, Spence and Oliver*

Cheryl's daughter Meredith and her girls - Vanessa and Ricardina

CHAPTER 33

My Brothers and Myself

My brothers and I were close, and because I didn't have any sisters, I was always so happy to see them and to talk with them.

When Ron and Cecile were living in Abbotsford, Ron and my brothers Murray and Eugene had a business called Reimer Enterprises. They built the Polar Avenue acreages project, Lake Estates, Alameda Courts, and Plateau Estates. They may have done other projects as well.

Cecile taught my grandchildren in Abbotsford in the French immersion course. When they sold their home to Gordon and Robbie Holloway on Plateau Estates, they moved to North Vancouver. They had a lovely place near Capilano Canyon.

I didn't see Ron that much after he left North Vancouver with his wife Cecile. They moved to Shetiak, New Brunswick, where Cecile had lots of family in the area and so she became close to her nephews and nieces. It was nice for her, as they never had any children of their own.

Ron was Ed and Don Quast's partner for a short time when they lived in Vancouver. The fellows bought Ron out when he moved to Shetiak.

Ron was so meticulous in his bookkeeping and when we both had shares in a company on the Vancouver Stock Exchange. He was so honest and diligent and we appreciated him so much.

After they left New Brunswick, they later moved back to Parksville, and I think they enjoy the weather better there.

Eugene and Ed were partners in a few ventures called Lake Estates. He was absolutely a scrupulous partner. He kept such good records and eventually we sold our ventures, which included five houses in Parksville and some other ventures.

Eugene was so cognoscente of other people that were paralyzed in one way or another that he would visit patients in GF Strong Rehabilitation Center in Vancouver every Thursday. Sometimes he would take the fellows out to a hockey game or do some other activities with them.

One of the patients there was Rick Hanson, who would later on become a world-class athlete and would do an around-the-world trip in his wheelchair. Gene rode in his wheelchair with him on the final lap into Vancouver from Chilliwack.

He also met Terry Fox who was running across Canada for awareness for cancer research. They all played wheelchair basketball and went to lots of tournaments together.

The three of them became good buddies and worked out together in Eugene's gym that he had built in his home on Polar Avenue in Abbotsford. Gene really became active in sports. He would wheel around Mount Lehman area for twenty-six miles every Saturday. The route he took had many hills on it.

I once asked Gene if he ever remembered walking. He told me, "No". I asked him if he ever wondered what it would be like.

He told me that he wouldn't trade his disability to be able-bodied.

He said to me, "If I wasn't disabled, I would never have won all the medals that I have. I would never have traveled all over the world. I would never have met the Queen or had an audience with the Pope."

He never regretted his life, even though he walked with crutches his whole life and suffered much pain.

Eugene was one of my heroes in my life. Despite his disabilities, he went on to win over one hundred medals in the Paralympics and other games in the world. He became the first disabled man to win Canada's Male Athlete of the Year in 1977. He also went on to have a middle school named after him, called the Eugene Reimer Middle School in Abbotsford. He also had an honoree doctorate of laws bestowed on him from the University of the Fraser Valley. He did all this while working as a draftsman and building many projects in the area. Eugene also had the Order of Canada bestowed on him by the Governor General of Canada. This is a very prestigious honor to have.

Because Gene lived in the same building as us in the Town Center Tower, we would see him often for dinner. He was such a sports advocate, that we would often watch hockey or baseball on our TV. He was so knowledgeable that Ed and I loved to hear all the statistics on sports he gave us.

My three brothers did a lot of building in Abbotsford. One of the properties was acreage pieces on Polar Avenue. I also mentioned Alameda Court and Lake Estates, which were condo developments.

It was a bad time in the years of about 1982 when interest rates went up to almost 18 to 20 percent and the economy was in a recession. We lost money on the project that we were in with Reimer Enterprises (on Alameda Court) but we never left any subtrades holding the "bag." We paid off every subtrade and all suppliers even though it ruined Gene's marriage and hurt Ron, Murray, and Gene financially.

I know of a lot of contractors that declared bankruptcies and just started a new company. From that point on, Gene could get any contractor or subtrade at a moment's notice, and they would do anything for the boys. I was so proud of my brother's reputation.

Early in 2008, Gene, who suffered from atrial fibrillation, had a procedure done in Vancouver General Hospital. His heart was racing so much that he sometimes had to call an ambulance. After being in hospital for about a week, he came home, went back to work, and suffered a stroke at work. He didn't get help soon enough and had bad damage done to his body. He was in Abbotsford Hospital for many months. His room was filled with drawings and cards from the Eugene Reimer Middle School students.

Gene always went to all the functions at the school, and the students really loved him. On June 9, 2008, my dear brother passed away. Rick Hanson spoke at his memorial service and the school named after him was closed that day. Later on after the service, everyone in our family went over to the school to see where he had a lot of his memorabilia and to talk to the students.

I miss Gene very much as do his children Jimmie, Kevin, and Lianne.

Murray and his wife Ingrid started a company called Reimer Financial in the Town Centre Tower that Ed and His friends built. He became very successful and later sold his company to Assante Financial. Murray still looks after my investments to this day.

After Murray sold his beautiful home at Plateau Estates, they moved to Parksville on Vancouver Island and built a beautiful home on some acreage right on the ocean. They also have a home in La Quinta in California. I visit them often and always have such a great time with them. Murray is so good to me.

Gordon and Diane, as I have mentioned, build Reimer Hardwoods.

Roger and his wife Ann met when Roger was going to a university in Washington. Roger was a school principal and Ann a teacher. I don't get to see Roger and Ann as much as I like because they live in Bellevue, Washington, in the USA. Roger and Ann have two children, Bryan and Melissa, and two new grandbabies.

It's a good thing Gene Reimer is a champion weightlifter, otherwise he would never be able to carry home the hardware he invariably wins in athletics. In Halifax at the Canada Games 10 days ago, Gene was named the best class three (the top category) athlete in the paraplegic division of the Canada Games. He won this trophy on the basis of his medal collection at the games. He brought in gold medals in weightlifting, pentathlon, archery and discus and took silvers in javelin, club throw and shot put. On the basis of his performance in Halifax, Gene was chosen to represent Canada in the paraplegic division of the Pan Am Games in Buenos Aires, Argentina in December.

Eugene.

CHAPTER 34

Keith

My youngest brother Keith was gay and I didn't know what that was when I was younger. I was so naïve.

The first time I found out about it was when Ed was vacuuming his room in a downstairs bedroom when Keith was living with us in Fort St. John while he attended grade twelve there.

He wanted to leave his environment in Abbotsford. He thought that maybe if he left there that he could change. He was one of the most handsome men that I have ever met.

While he was living with us, I was just home from a break from the Edmonton Hospital where I had gone for more surgeries. Keith worked in the Safeway grocery store bagging groceries after school. Ed noticed a book on homosexuality in his room and mentioned it to me.

He told me what it was about, so when Keith came home, we asked him about it. He said that he had tried so hard for years to ignore these feelings, and he was so torn up about it, and wondered if he could change.

I always noticed that he was different as a child, but thought that he just didn't like sports like the other guys. Ed and I so understood him and we loved him to pieces and would talk with him often about it.

Ed bought him a little MG convertible. He took it down to Vancouver. He entered nursing school and wanted to study physiology in order to better understand himself. Keith graduated from the School of Psychiatric Nursing in 1969

Keith was a beautiful man, not flamboyant in any way, but very sensitive. He met a young man named Ron. They became partners, owned a hairdressing shop in North Vancouver, sold that, and moved to Los Angeles. They had a successful business there. My brother Ron and Cecile had visited them in North Vancouver and became good friends with them.

My family, Cheryl, Bruce, and Kirk cared for them, as did my brothers, and accepted them with love. When the boys and Ed and I would visit them in LA, we would often go to the six flags Mountain museum and do other fun things in LA.

While they were there, it was around the time of everyone becoming aware of AIDS and the devastation that individuals were suffering from.

It was the era of when Rock Hudson "came out" and died. The disease was a mystery and everyone was so apprehensive about catching it.

While Ron and Keith were there, Keith confided to me that he was HIV positive and Ron was too. We didn't know what that meant, but Ron died from AIDS and Keith developed the full-blown disease. When he told us about it, we were so shocked.

He came up to see us, and I remember he stayed with us at Plateau Estates one night, and then my darling brother Gordon and Diane offered their basement apartment for Keith to live in.

Gordon and Diane had built a beautiful home on forty acres, which had a daylight basement, a pond, and horse riding stables. Their home was a state of the art estate. We were so appreciative of them doing this, but we were all so afraid of the disease and paranoid of touching anything that he had touched.

Remember, this was the early 1980s and no one knew much about how this was transferred.

Gordon and Diane are the most caring couple that you will ever meet. They were so kind to do this for Keith.

One day, my brothers and I were sitting around the recreation room in the downstairs area. Cheryl, who was in medical school, came in to visit. She walked over to Keith, put her arms around Keith, and hugged him and told him how much she loved him and kissed him on the cheek.

We were shocked. She later told us that we could not catch the disease this way.

Keith lived at Gordon and Diane's home for a short time, but wanted to go back to LA because all his friends were there. Eugene took him to the Bellingham airport for a first-class ticket back home. We asked him to let us know when he got home.

We didn't hear from him, so Gordon and I started phoning the hospitals, and found him in Cedar Sinead Hospital where the doctors told us he was very sick. All his organs were shutting down and he would never leave the hospital.

The doctors asked us if we should let him die, and Murray, Gordon, and I made the decision to take him off life support. It was a terrible time for us, but Keith had asked me to please not keep him alive if this should happen. I promised him that I would honor his wishes. My dear brother died September 24, 1991, at forty-six years of age.

He also said he had made his peace with God, and asked to be cremated and his body sent to Sumas, Washington.

He also asked me if my brothers and I could put some of his ashes in my mom's grave and some of them in the Skagit River where my dad died. He felt that he could unite our parents that way. I told him that it was just beautiful.

Gordon had a beautiful outdoor service on his estate for Keith with all our families there, and later on we went out to the Skagit, just my brothers and I and our spouses.

We went to Mom's grave put a few ashes in it and a few roses, and then went out to the Skagit River. We each threw a rose into the river after we put the ashes in there. It was beautiful. He was such a wonderful, caring, and sensitive man and we all loved him dearly.

So, that was the history of my brothers and now I will talk a little bit about Ed's family and mine and our lives with our wonderful friends.

Keith.

CHAPTER 35

Abbotsford

As I mentioned earlier, we moved to Plateau Estates. Our very best friends were Ernie and Ardis Janzen. We did so many things together with them. Ed and Ernie would "run" many miles, and because I worked for Ernie doing all the financials for the doctors, we became great friends.

We would spend every Christmas Eve together after we had gone to church. We both joined the Sevenoaks Alliance Church in 1969. We got together with other couples and formed a group called "Homebuilders" which were all couples our age.

In the 1970s, twin brothers Ralph and Lou Sutera came to Abbotsford to hold evangelistic meetings in our church. They planned to stay for ten days.

We had agreed that they could stay with us for the ten days, and they stayed in Cheryl's room and Cher slept on an air mattress in our room.

Well, the ten days ended up being five weeks. We had such a huge revival in our city, that dozens of people were committing their lives to Christ, and also rededicating their lives.

I remember the first day they arrived. The pastor dropped them off at our place. Lou immediately went to the fridge and Ralph told us our pastor was "carnal." We were quite taken aback, but our church really was.

My aunt Lou who had just moved to Abbotsford from Alberta and felt so sorry for us that we had these people staying with us for so long that she would come over sometimes but would never go to church. We lent the Suteras our white Cadillac sports car and they made quite an impression, with their black hair and long dark coats driving in a white Cadillac. It was quite a sight.

People from the church really brought over meals and were very helpful, but the brothers said that they would prefer to just stay in our place rather than moving around, so we just kept them at our place. One of the phenomena was the "after parties" which people held in their homes after the church services. Many people became Christians at these parties, where the Suteras would talk to people to help them believe.

One night, my aunt Lou came over and because she was always a "party girl" she wanted to get in on the party. We were all talking about giving our lives to God, and she said that no way would she ever do that.

She said that all Christians were sad sacks and cried all the time, and she wanted to laugh and have fun. Finally, after talking until about two AM, she said she wanted to pray to become a Christian, but she didn't want to be sad. The first thing she did was cry, because she was so happy.

Lou had lived a very wild life and was an alcoholic and a chain smoker. She said that the addiction of alcohol left her immediately that evening. The Suteras included her in their visits when they went to schools and city rallies so that she could give her testimony of a changed life. One day, she felt it wasn't good to talk and smoke, so she gave up smoking too.

Lou later went on to volunteer with Campus Crusade (now called Power to Change) and started "Entertaining with a Purpose" parties. Many people came to know the Lord through these parties.

We would always make guests aware of the talks that would be given.

We would have appetizers, punch, and dinner, and then a couple would tell how they had come to know Christ, and guests would be given a chance to fill out a card on their thoughts of the evening. People were always told what would happen when they were invited. Then we would have dessert and lots of laughs.

Lou later on married Neil Wiebe who's wife had died a few years earlier. They had a fun life, entertaining and traveling the world. They were married for eight and a half years, before he died of a heart attack.

Some of the other vacations we took were to Nashville and we liked to go to Manhattan every other year, usually during the end of November and beginning of December until Ed got sick. I had cut my brothers hair when they were teenagers, and cut Ed's hair all his life. He liked the way I styled it. So, later on Neil had me cut his hair also.

CHAPTER 36

Town Centre Tower

After living in Vancouver for two years in False Creek, which I absolutely loved, Ed and his friends John Voth and Don Quast decided they wanted to build a beautiful high-rise tower on a piece of property we owned on South Fraser Way in Abbotsford.

We built an eighteen-story gorgeous building with a glass roof. We started to get financing and sales for the building. The HSBC gave us the financing. Ed did the major part of the financial part. John put lots of money into it, and Don did the sales, mostly out of the car dealership. John built the building. He did a magnificent job.

To this day, Town Centre Tower is the nicest building in Abbotsford.

Ed wanted me to come back to Abbotsford to live in it as he thought it would be better if all of us partners lived in it. I really didn't want to leave Vancouver, as I was so happy there with Ed living on Beach Avenue surrounded by the water of False Creek. I wasn't keen on moving.

We had a lovely place but Ed promised me that if we moved there, I could do anything I wanted in the penthouse. He felt that the building would sell better if the original investors lived in it. So, Ed, who can get his own way, in a nice gentle way, convinced me to move. The building had forty-seven suites ranging from 1,300 square feet to 2,600 square feet. It was all air-conditioned. John and Emily Voth and us shared the penthouses, which had a large loft, and many outdoor patios. Indoor space was approximately 3,010 square feet. On our side, I made beautiful brick planters and had all the wonderful flowers that I loved, planted.

We needed 50 percent of the units sold for the HSBC financing. So, my brother Eugene bought a suite. Kirk, our son; Devron, Don and Sheryl's son; John and Emily's daughter and her husband all bought a suite. My aunt Lou bought a suite, as well as Fred Rempel who bought two suites. Lawrence Friesen, and the Martens each bought a suite. The Martens, Friesens, and Fred Rempel each had a small share.

So, with the principal partners, we had enough sales. John and Emily lived across the street from Ed and I at Plateau Estates, so we have been neighbors for thirty-five to thirty-six years. I treasure these friends and they became one of our dearest friends as a couple.

CHAPTER 37

Ed's Ireland Trip (1992)

Ed was on the Matsqui Police Board of Governors, having been appointed by the BC government to serve. A really good friend of his, Dr. Craig Seaton, invited him to go to Ireland with him and a few alumni to visit and intended to go to Dublin and Belfast, on a reconciliation tour. They did visit a prison in Belfast, and Ed was amazed at the amount of tension in the cities. This was before the whole situation in Ireland was neutralized.

As visiting dignitaries in a new county always brought gifts, Craig asked me if I had a piece of art that they could give as gifts to their hosts in each city they visited.

I had done a watercolor of "Butterflies in Belfast." This piece depicted the emergence of a cocoon, and of a beautiful creature coming out of the old and now flying out to a new life. Craig and Ed gave away many prints of this piece. The president of Ireland, Mary McCree, in Dublin, asked Craig if she could have the original painting to hang in Government House in Dublin.

She said she would like to meet the artist, but I could not go on a subsequent trip that Craig took to give it to her. I was truly honored and humbled.

It was during the conflict between Belfast and Dublin. On one occasion, Ed witnessed a person putting on old clothes. When asked why, he replied that he was going to get "knee-capped."

Apparently, if one had disobeyed the rules, this is how they dealt with it. Ed was shocked.

As an aside, it is noted that some of the best orthopedic surgeons in the world came from Ireland.

Ed always wanted to return to Ireland, as he said it was so "green" and beautiful. He wanted to show this beautiful country to me.

While Ed was in Ireland, the HSBC pulled our financing. They said that the building going up across the street was a better risk. John told Ed that he had already dug the hole, so Ed came home a week early to find another bank. The Bank of Montreal agreed to finance us, but Ed had to put in more cash. It was lucky that we had it then.

I can't stress hard enough how very competent John is at building high-rises. He poured over every document and plan for hours, days, and months. He built it on budget and made every homeowner happy with any changes they might want. Our suite was the last finished, as we wanted everyone to be happy with his or her apartments first before our suite was done.

I was probably the hardest to please, as I really like interior design and had my own ideas. John was amazing and complied with my every wish.

Don Quast did an amazing job of sales, and we had soon sold all the units, in the nicest building in Abbotsford to this day. The Quasts and the Voths still live there. I just moved out in May of 2015 after Ed got sick.

After Ed sold Rempel Bros. and his contract was finished, he had a home office built in the high-rise. It was all done beautifully, like a gentleman's office, with walls of molding of the highest-grade wood and bookshelves all around the room for his thousands of hardcover books that he had read. Ed was an avid reader, all nonfiction. He loved books on history, biographies, and business.

My art studio was built in the loft. I liked this as it had glass railings around it, looking down on the suite, and so I never felt closed in. There were three beautiful patios around it that I could utilize. It was a wonderful studio and I do miss it today.

We lived there for twenty-two years, saw many changes, but were very happy there. We had an incredible three hundred-degree view of the valley and Mount Baker with floor-to-ceiling windows in an air conditioned building.

During the time we lived there, Ernie, with two partners, built a lovely new medical building next door to our building.

A few years after it was built, there was an arson fire in it. It was totally burned down. It was absolutely devastating for the doctors. This was the time that Ernie had been diagnosed with CLL and it certainly exasperated his stress level. He decided to rebuild it from new again with the insurance money. I think it was good for him to have a focus on this new beautiful building. It was certainly very hard on him though, while being so sick. Ernie suffered for four years until he passed away on August 31, 1998.

Ernie always told Ed that they were very close to finding a cure for CLL. But it would be too late for him. It is interesting that Ernie's running buddy, Ed, developed and contracted the same disease. We rented an apartment in Vancouver for a year and Ed went to chemo in Vancouver for a year, never developed a side effect, and was cured totally. It was just a short few years after had Ernie died.

CHAPTER 38

Travels

We did quite a bit of travel with our family when they were growing up. We used to spend some days at Sun Valley, Idaho, with the kids skiing. We would go to Palm Springs later, a lot, with our group of friends, the Voths, the Quasts, and Hank and Elaine Funk.

We would all rent condos around a pool and the boys and later our grandchildren would swim, go to Disneyland, and do so many fun things.

Cheryl was away doing medicine, but we were able to take Derek and Meredith sometimes.

Other times when the boys got older, we would take a friend for each of them to our trips to Hawaii and Las Vegas, etc. Gerald, because he didn't have a father, would often accompany Bruce, and some of the other cousins would come also. One year Cathie Reimer joined us.

One trip that we did was to the island of Kauai with my brothers and their children. It was so much fun because the kids would all hang out together and us adults could have a great time. We picked Poi Poi beach as it was smaller at the time and the kids couldn't get lost or get into trouble.

One trip to Maui, our kids and some cousins, Gerald, and others along with Ed all took the Maui scuba diving courses and so they got their certificates also. I couldn't because I had asthma. These courses proved very valuable on other water-related trips we took.

Ed and I would go to a lot of conventions. Ed was always trying to find more efficient ways to improve his company. He spent every hour at them, gleaning all the information he could. One trip, Murray Blackham and Jack Rempel and their wives joined Ed and I and it was so good. One time when we were in Houston, the guys all bought cowboy boots and hats.

Often, when Ed and I were away for a few days, we would tack a few extra days on and fly to interesting places that were close to where we were going, for example Nashville, Washington, DC, Atlanta, and so on. We always made these interesting and fun times. We would hire a sitter for the boys while we were away, so that was good.

Ed and I loved to go to New York in the fall near Christmas time. We enjoyed the theatre a lot, Ed enjoyed going to the Museums with me. My favorite was the MOMA. Ed was so patient, allowing me as much time as I wanted.

CHAPTER 39

Our First Cruise

O ne Christmas Eve, Ed, Don Quast, and John Voth surprised all of us girls with a cruise to the Caribbean. I was so excited to look forward to taking our first cruise.

We left on February 2, 1991.

Well, we were on our first day out of Florida, and went to the island of Martinique. We spent the day having so much fun, sightseeing and shopping. The waters were so lovely. Ed loved to run, and he told me that he was going to go ashore and go for a run after we had returned to the ship.

I had a migraine, so I laid down for a short time. I suddenly felt the ship moving. I thought Ed must be back, but he wasn't in the room. I went to the back of the ship and Ed wasn't there, so I phoned John and Don to ask them if they had seen Ed. They said they hadn't seen him.

I know that when Ed goes on a run, the first thing he does is to have a shower when he returns. I immediately felt a panic that Ed had missed the boat. I was sitting in my room crying with the door open when a porter walked by and asked me what was wrong. I told him that my husband had gone for a run and wasn't back. He replied, "Oh, yes, there are lots of women on Martinique and he probably ran off with one of them" I told him no, that he was jogging. He called the captain to come down to talk to me.

When I told Don and John, they told me that if we hadn't heard anything by morning, that they would hire a small plane to go look for him. Apparently, there were winding narrow roads and the guys thought that maybe he got hit by a car or mugged by someone.

Nowadays, the ship would know if anyone missed the ship, but then, all Ed had on him was a Princess Cruise Ship card. I looked in the safe, and his wallet was there, his passport, his watch, and all his money.

The captain came down to talk to me, and told me that we were out of satellite range, so they had no way of knowing what had happened to him. About midnight, he said he would call the ships agent in Martinique.

Meanwhile, Ed got lost running up the hills on the island, and finally made his way down to the shore, to see the ship heading out to sea. He had no money, no credit card, and no passport. It was now about six PM and starting to get dark.

He saw an office that looked like a ship agent's office. So, he went up to it just as they were closing. When he told them his story, they said they would contact the ship, but that they would try to take him to the next island by plane. The ship was out of contact range until midnight and could not be contacted before then.

The ship's agent phoned St. Thomas, but St. Thomas would not take Ed, because they were wary of him. The Gulf War going on then. They asked if he looked like an Iraqi, but the agent told him no, he had sandy-colored hair. They wouldn't take him, so they told Ed the only possible way he could join the cruise was maybe St. Maarten, which was a Dutch island and they were more lenient, but he would have to wait for two days.

They then flew him to Guadeloupe where he slept on the beach, and then to St. Maarten, where they said they would take him without a passport.

Ed stayed in a sleazy room at Joseph's guesthouse until the ship arrived in his sweaty t-shirt and shorts. He forgot his contact lens on the bedside table, so we got to see the place the next day.

Meanwhile, the captain told me about midnight that Ed would catch up with Myrtle-Anne in two days, but that he was safe. I was so relieved.

When Ed arrived at the dock, he immediately boarded the ship, hugged me, and had a shower with two days' grime to wash off.

We went ashore and had a great time buying some jewelry and souvenirs. Ed had a gold bracelet on his wrist when he was lost, and felt that was his only asset.

While Ed was on the island, Ed knew that I would be very worried, so he phoned collect to Cheryl's home. Meredith answered the phone and he asked to talk to her parents. Meredith told him that her mom and dad were out, so Ed said to give them a message. "Tell them that I am okay, and that I will catch up with Myrtle-Anne in two days." They chuckled about that later.

When Barry and Cheryl got home, she gave them the message and they both surmised what had happened.

Later, when we got home, Ed told me not to tell anyone about him missing the ship. However, when I went to the Safeway, four people asked me how Ed was and giggled, I knew that the story was out there. Everyone knew. Ed said that he didn't think the office staff knew. I told him that everyone knew, and his office staff were just too polite to say anything. Poor Ed.

It was quite a story. We had a six-day cruise and Ed only had a four-day cruise. Later on, Ed had a lot of laughs about this story. He was a good sport and thought it was funny later.

CHAPTER 40

The Orient

On February 23, 1984, Ed and I went on a business trip to Taiwan with some government officials and business people from British Columbia to help foster a relationship with Taiwan between business and government.

It was an incredible trip. Bill Kerkhoff was on this trip also. Everyone treated us so well. We stayed in the lovely United Hotel along with the delegation from BC. We then went on to Taipei, and did some shopping and 'sightseeing.

We ate wonderful food, and met many dignitaries of each city. The people were wonderful. We often saw people out on the streets selling their goods, while their children went to school six days a week.

When Ed sold his share of Rempel Bros. in 1988, he promised to stay on for three more years as president. During that time, he implemented an RRSP plan for all the employees with the company matching contributions. He also asked for some time off to take a trip to Hong Kong with our friends, the Quasts. We planned to stop in Hawaii briefly on our way home. So, on February 26, 1990, we flew to Hong Kong and stayed at the Regent Hotel, which was very beautiful, but didn't have heat in it.

I had just lost quite a bit of weight, so I had a hard time keeping warm. We had a wonderful time, toured a lot, met Don's cousin

Everett Krohn and his wife, Eliza. We also visited some tailors and the guys had suits and other clothes handmade for them. Beautiful suits were made in just a few days. We went to a Mongolian bar-beque and had wonderful food the whole time we were there. The stores were so modern and the hotels and restaurants were beautiful. We went to the Golden Mile and the Stanley Market, which was fun. They took us to the yacht club, which was fun as Ed and I are members of the Royal Vancouver Yacht Club and we had reciprocal privileges with other yacht clubs in the world.

On March 10, we left for Maui to spend some time in Hawaii before traveling home. We had some beautiful rooms and had a great time, but Ed had to go back to Canada early, because we were having some problems with the manager of one of our companies, so we left a few days early for home. Wherever we traveled, Ed always kept in touch by phone.

CHAPTER 41

Ed's Birthdays

Cheryl and I planned a celebration for Ed's seventieth birthday. We thought it was a significant landmark so we decided to make it "black tie optional." We hired a paddle-wheeler boat in Coal Harbor in Vancouver.

We decided to make it a fun dinner cruise all around False Creek and back. We also decided to make it a surprise for Ed. Ed loves surprises.

I did one for his sixtieth birthday in our penthouse where the boys and I presented him with his old Marconi Radio that he inherited from his family. I had it all reconditioned and we found some old original parts in the US. He was absolutely delighted with it.

On his fiftieth birthday, Jackie Rempel hung a big sign on the office building outside of the Rempel Bros. office, saying "Happy Half a Hundred Uncle Eddie." Funnily, Ed didn't notice it when he drove up until one of the secretaries mentioned it to him. He loved it and got quite a kick out of it.

I would like to go back to the seventieth birthday surprise party. I invited about ninety people. Eighty people were able to come. I invited all the business managers that he was involved with. I also invited close family members and his close friends. I also invited the persons serving on the same boards he was on. I felt this party was for him and so it was mostly for people he was involved with. It turned out to be a beautiful evening.

I decided that we would stay at the Bayshore Inn the night before. It was only a short walk for us to the boat. I told him that we had plans to meet Cheryl and her friend Tony at the yacht club for dinner on his birthday, June 4. "But first," I said, "why don't we walk down the pier and look at the boats."

He said, "No, I don't want to be late for dinner." I tried to persuade him that we had time, but Ed, who was always punctual and never late, was alarmed. Cheryl phoned me on my cell phone and said that everyone was on the boat and we should come now.

I told Ed that Cheryl was running a little late so we had time to walk down to the pier. As we got near to the pier, Grace and Ray McCarthy met us. Ray was not feeling well so decided to just say hello to Ed rather than join us.

While we were standing there, people were all singing Happy Birthday. Ed said, "It's someone's birthday." He looked stunned.

I said, "It's your birthday today."

He replied, "What a coincidence."

Everyone was shouting, "Surprise!" He still didn't catch on until we boarded the boat. He was so delighted to see everyone there.

We greeted our guests with champagne or fruit juice. We sailed off and everyone mingled until we served them with a hot dinner. While we were sailing, my nephew Jackie, who worked with Ed, gave a speech, roasting him about him at work.

Hank Funk also roasted him royally, mainly about politics. He was so funny and Ed enjoyed every minute of it. Cheryl gave her "top ten" things she loved about her dad, and Kirk told him that he had won the lottery when he got Ed for a dad.

It was a wonderful evening. I am so glad that we did it. Even though it was costly for me, I wanted it to be special for Ed, and it was a nice way to entertain all our friends and family.

Ed was always so generous with gifts of flowers (always red roses) and with jewelry for me. He often bought items from Lee's and from Birks. One day I told him that he didn't need to buy me anymore as

I had lots. He looked sad, so a few years later, I told him it was okay to buy me more. He looked so happy and the next occasion, I got another lovely piece of jewelry. He was such a kind and gentle man. Ed was so fastidious about his grooming and his clothing. He always looked so classy.

Ed 72—Before he got sick.

CHAPTER 42

Other Places

M arch 21 to April 1, 1990, we went to Banff for an ICBA conference.

January 1991, we went to the World of Concrete in Las Vegas with Bruce who was married to Melody and the Waldens, who were friends of ours in the USA.

February 14, 1990, we went to Victoria for the Annual Policeman's Awards. We stayed in the Harbor Tower Hotel. Ed was on the Board of Governors of the Abbotsford Police for four years. He really enjoyed his time on that board. He traveled around the city sometimes in a police car to see what the officers had to put up with. He found it an interesting board to be on. During his tenure, they hired a new police chief, Barry Daniels, who became our friend.

Ed was on the Canadian Board of Governors for the Robert Schuler ministries for ten years and we often visited Los Angeles for a meeting. The grounds of the Crystal Cathedral were beautiful. Ed left just before they were having problems with that ministry. The grandson Bobby Schuler is now the pastor and he is a great guy.

We would also visit my brother Keith and his partner Ron who lived down there.

Ed in happier days.

CHAPTER 43

Austria

M eredith, Cheryl, and I decided that we would save our money, from gifts, Mother's Day, birthdays, Christmas, etc., and put it into an account for a trip to Vienna.

August 25, 1991 to September 1, 1991, we were in Vienna. It was right after Meredith graduated from Simon Fraser University.

Cher had a friend, Elisabeth Hruby, who lived there and had invited us to visit. Cher stayed with Elisabeth and Meredith and I stayed in a hotel. The hotels we stayed in were the Sacher-Wein and the Hotel Imperial.

We had a wonderful time visiting the museums—Belvedere, where I enjoyed Vermeer's "Blue Artist" model.

It was the two hundredth anniversary of Mozart's death. We went to Vienna State Opera and heard music by Strauss and Mozart.

On August 29, we went to Salzburg, which was three hours from Vienna on the Autobahn. It is a beautiful place. Everyone is so friendly. Our favorite gallery was the Klimt museum. The paintings there were incredible, and he quickly became our favorite modern artist. We bought prints of Klimt's work to frame.

CHAPTER 44

Maui

December 25, 1991 to January 10, 1992, we went on a Maui family vacation. We stayed at the Kannapolis Ali Hotel. Cheryl, Barry, Derek, Meredith, Bruce, Kirk as well as Gerald were there.

Everyone took scuba diving courses except me, as I had asthma. They all got their Maui diving certificates. It was a great time, but we all agreed that we would rather be home for Christmas. Santa coming up on a boat to give presents to the people on the shore didn't compensate for our times at home at Christmas.

Ed and I were in Maui for three weeks, and the children were there for two weeks. After the second week, Ed and I got a little antsy and wanted to get back home. We weren't that good on long holidays.

We did a lot of sightseeing and some shopping.

The last vacation that Ed and I took was on Maui. He was starting to get really sick, so I told our children that this would be our last vacation.

CHAPTER 45

New York Trips

In December of 1992 and subsequent visits to New York for a few days, we would visit the TV shows that were there.

We saw Kathie Lee and Regis, Joan Rivers, Radio City Music Hall, Letterman, and many others, as well as touring the museums and art galleries. One of my favorite galleries was the Frick Museum. We would often go to TKTS to get half price tickets for the theater. Ed commented to me one day, "I can't believe you got me up at five AM to go see Regis," which is about two AM our time. If you knew Ed, he was always so accommodating and so easygoing.

We spent many three-day trips to New York and enjoyed so many plays, as well as visiting the MOMA. In this Museum of Modern Art, I got to see all the modern painters that I idealized. In particular, I liked Jackson Pollack and so many more American artists. Ed and I loved to walk the streets and visit great restaurants. We did lots of shopping on Fifth Avenue and took the horse buggy tour of Central Park.

We saw lots of places that individuals lived in, like Jackie Kennedy and Donald Trump. We visited the Trump Tower, which was lovely. We also attended the large hall where the Rockets worked out and saw the performances every year of the Christmas Special at Radio City Music Hall.

An interesting aside was that we met Donald Trump twice. The first time was in the lobby of the Plaza Hotel, when he was with a group of men. He greeted us with a handshake. It was a very pleasant encounter. This was during the time of his marriage to Marla Maples.

The second time we met him was at the Le Cirque restaurant. Ed and I decided that we didn't want to see the lighting of the Christmas tree in Rockefeller Center as we had seen it a number of times, so we would just go for dinner.

The restaurant was quite empty as most people were at the tree lighting. We sat down at a nice table and ordered our dinner. Donald and Melania Trump came in and sat at the table next to us. When we got up to leave, Donald stood up and reached out to shake Ed's hand. Ed introduced himself and Donald asked him what business he was in. Ed mentioned "gold mining," which was something he was focused on at the time. Donald said, "That's a good thing." I told Mr. Trump that his wife is very beautiful and he replied to Ed that his wife was very beautiful too.

The encounter was so nice and he seemed to be so nice and classy and not at all like the person one sees on TV. It is interesting, that as the writing of this, he has been elected as President of the United States.

Later, on November 29 to December 2, 2000, while Ed and John Voth took a trip to India, Emily and I went to New York and stayed at the Marriot. We had such a good time. We were given complimentary desserts which were fabulous at Le Cirque restaurant, when they found out we were tourists.

One day when we were having coffee in the Trump Tower coffee shop, some water came down on Emily. The cleaner above had spilt his clean water on us. We were upset, but they paid for our lunch. Poor Emily was all wet on her new leather outfit. Thankfully, she was a good sport and we laughed about it later.

We walked a lot and saw a few good shows. We also went to David Wilkerson's church. The congregation was so large and packed out, but when the ushers saw that we were new, they took us to the front, and regular parishioners gave us their seats. They were so nice.

BRUSHSTROKES OF LIFE: AN AUTOBIOGRAPHY

On one of our trips, we were invited to Hans and Anne Spenst's son Rick's wedding in Brooklyn. It was such a lovely wedding, so different from what we were used to, but beautiful.

November 29 to December 2004, we traveled to New York with Cheryl. We had the best time ever with Cher. We did a lot of shopping on Fifth Avenue, especially at St. John's ladies wear. We went to Ground Zero, the Whitney museum, and the Museum of Modern Art. The MOMA was showing Klimt, Pollack, Rauschenberg, and other famous artists. We did all the usual, Letterman, Regis, Radio City Christmas, Le Circ, the Rainbow room and had wonderful dinners. We had three fantastic days in New York with Cheryl.

CHAPTER 46

Other Trips

March 26 to 28, 1993, we were invited to Government House in Ottawa for a special dinner with the prime minister and cabinet. When we got to the Four Seasons Hotel in Toronto, I found that I was having a really hard time breathing. I had developed an asthmatic attack.

We were to carry on to Ottawa where we had reservations at the Westin Hotel. However, I ended up in the hospital in emergency in ICU on a ventilator. I was so sad to miss Ottawa. I got out of hospital, but I was not allowed to fly for five days, to return home. We left directly home to Vancouver. We did meet up with Gerry and Gloria Mudge, who were living in Toronto.

December 30 to January 14, 1995, our husbands gave us Christmas presents again of a back-to-back eastern and western Caribbean cruise. Don and Sheryl, John and Emily, and Hank and Elaine joined us. On board, Ed and I took a few dancing lessons. It was great to go through the locks between the Atlantic and the Pacific oceans.

While we were down in Palm Desert on March 10 to 20, 1995, we got a call from a realtor who really wanted to sell our apartment in Vancouver. She had buyers lined up, so we completed the sale over the phone, with faxes being sent back and forth.

Because we were now living in the TCT, we had been renting the apartment out for about five years, and weren't using it. It was a lovely 1,700 square foot suite right on the beach in False Creek. I really wish we had not sold it, however, we were starting our life in Abbotsford again.

Myrtle-Anne, Meredith and Cheryl – Vienna and Austria trip

CHAPTER 47

Paris, France

May 24, 1995, Meredith, Cheryl, and I again saved up for a trip. We went to Paris until June 1. "Les Trois Femmes." Meredith had done her law degree in Moncton, a French university, where she studied British law. She was so proficient in this language that we decided that she would be our interpreter, Cheryl would be our travel guide, and I would be the arts and architecture guide.

We stopped in Toronto to visit our good friends, the Mudges.

When we arrived in Paris, we stayed at the Hotel College De France, a modest but nice hotel.

We did the city tour the first day, and saw the Opera House. There was ideal shopping on Rue de St. Honore. We did a tour of the Louvre. It was excellent and very emotional for me to be able to see the Venus De Milo statue in person.

I was reminded again of the funny story of when we lived at Plateau Estates. I had completed a lot of ceramics and did a ceramic of the Venus de Milo. A funny aside to that was that when Kirk's friends would come to our home, they told him that there was a naked woman in the bathroom. Kirk would reply, "That's only Venus De Milo," and would laugh.

We visited Napoleon's private apartments and the gorgeous gardens.

Highlights of the Louvre tour were:

1. Le Bruins—four canvasses … Battle of Arbela
2. La Tour—Portrait of Marquis De Pompadour
3. Victory of Samothrace—winged marble
4. Mona Lisa—Leonardo de Vinci, most expensive piece.
5. Veronese—wedding feast
6. Louis David—coronation of David and Josephine

The next day we visited four museums. The best sculptures were in the Musee D Orsey, which previously was an old railroad station. Some highlights were:

- Voltaire's Inferno—Father and four sons dying of hunger, and stressed.
- Degas—Ballet Dancers
- Cezanne and Mary Cassatt paintings.
- Orson Wells—filming of Trial
- Opera House Model
- Renoir—two girls at the piano

Picasso Museum had a large collection of his work during the blue period, pink cubism, surrealist art. There was such a large collection including seven different media, which were used.

Musee de L'Orange. It was the Impressionist period, where we saw the works of Monet's Water Lilies, "Nymphaies," which were in two large rooms with four panels each. We saw works by Manet, Monet, and Renoir. The architecture was beautiful.

We then went to the Musee Rodin in an elegant townhouse and with English gardens. The sculptures were wonderful.

The next day we went to Sacre de Coeur, which is a church at the highest point, followed by shopping at the Gallerie La Fayette. We saw so many beautiful items.

On May 30, we went on the metro to Versailles.

Cheryl was our guide and fell asleep on the metro. I awoke her a few times when we were near what I thought was our stop, but she said no and fell asleep again. We finally ended up at the end of the line at the Belgium border. So we turned around and went to our proper stop. It was lovely to tour the countryside and we had a lot of good laughs about that.

We toured the wonderful palace and the grounds. We toured the king's chamber and Marie Antoinette's apartments.

Later we met up with Francois and Bertrand Grisel, who were friends with Meredith. They lived in Versailles. We had dinner with them, and Meredith stayed with them for another few weeks after Cheryl and I left for home.

On our last day in Paris, we went to Musee De Marmottan, which was converted from a beautiful mansion to a museum. We enjoyed Monet, Renoir, but especially Pissarro. The grounds were wonderful.

Next, we toured Musee d'art Moderne de LeParis. We enjoyed Marc Chagall, the Russian years, which were the first fifteen years of his career. His Jewish theater creations were wonderful.

On our last night, we did the canal cruise and city tour. Lights of Paris were wonderful.

CHAPTER 48

Palm Desert

In March 10 to 20, 1995, we met Gerry and Ursula Jones at the Marriott time-share in Palm Desert. It was great to watch the tennis matches and a thrill to see Agassi and Sampras play. At the time, they were rated number 1 and number 2 in the world.

Gerry passed away when we lived at Town Center Tower. It was so sad for Ursula, and she moved to Vancouver shortly after that. I do see her in Vancouver and she has remarried a nice man named Gerald. I see Ursula and Gerald quite a bit in Vancouver.

March 26 to May 12, 1996, the Voths, Quasts, Funks, and us stayed at the Palm Valley Country Club in Palm Desert. We had so much fun swimming and shopping. We ate at great restaurants and drove around to all the sites.

March 16 to April 1, 2002, we were in Palm Springs with John and Emily. We stayed at Cathedral Canyon Country Club, went to Los Angeles, and saw the JP Getty Museum. We attended the Southwest Community Church Easter Service at the Tennis Center. Twelve thousand people were there to hear John Tesh. The Cliff House was one of our favorite restaurants.

We had many other trips with our children and also alone to the desert in later years.

Ed and I thought about buying a home in one of the resorts there, however, we decided that we didn't want to be limited to only visiting the Desert.

Ed and I always enjoy the Desert. We have numerous friends who have homes there.

Gary and Laurie Siemens have a great home in Palm Desert.

Murray and Ingrid have a beautiful model home in the Trilogy development in La Quinta and Paul and Darlene have a lovely home in the La Quinta area.

Many of our friends live in the Outdoor Resorts on 48th Avenue in La Quinta.

CHAPTER 49

Cruising

September 6 to 26, 2003, Paul and Darlene and Ed and I took a cruise on the Royal Caribbean cruise line to the Mediterranean. We started in Barcelona, and our favorite places were Nice, Capri, and Florence. Monaco was interesting and Rome was great for shopping.

We took nine tours including seeing Pompeii, which was excellent. We then left for London for five days, where we met up with Christopher Howard. We got home just in time for surgery on my left foot scheduled for October 6. Paul always teased me about my funny shoes on the trip. We had a lovely time with them.

Another cruise we took was with Don and Sheryl and Hank and Elaine for twelve days to Jamaica, Grand Cayman, Costa Rica, and to the Panama Canal. Then back to Freeport in the Bahamas and to Fort Lauderdale. Hank and Elaine Funk and Ed and I had a wonderful time touring the countryside and having lovely lunches.

We also went to Alaska on a cruise with sixteen people. The Mudges and their friends from Toronto joined us. Along with us were the Funks, the Quasts, Ardis Janzen, my aunt Lou, and others. I did lots of sketching of the glaciers.

Myrtle-Anne and Ed cruise

Cruise—Don & Sheryl Quast, Hank & Elaine Funk, John & Emily
Voth and Ed & Myrtle-Anne on the left.

CHAPTER 50

Other Places

We also spent some weekends in Penticton with our friends at the Lakeside Hotel from when the children were small. Bruce and Melody and the girls joined us when they were living in Kelowna. I remember one time when we were there, and the adults all decided to go for dinner.

The kids were all in two rooms, and we told them to just order room service. Well, they would phone down for a Coke or some fries but never at the same time, so when John and I went to pay the bill at the end, there was an arm length of charges for each of us for separate item, and when the service charge for each item was added, it came up to a huge amount. We got a kick out of that. Mostly Kirk thought it was great. He would order a Coke and then half an hour later fries and so on it went. John and I looked at the bills for each of our rooms and were astonished but amused.

One of the times we were in Penticton, the children all went wind surfing in the air. Aretha was so light that the men had a hard time getting her down. We all enjoyed the shopping in Penticton.

We took our kids to Osoyoos when they were younger, but one day when I was swimming in the lake, I came across some feces and was alarmed. We stayed around the pool and wouldn't let the children go in the lake after that.

We did go to Kalamalka Lake in Vernon sometimes. The water was so blue. Our children loved these small vacations on the beaches.

CHAPTER 51

The Last Travels for Ed and Myself

I n the spring of 2009, Ed and I planned a trip to Palm Desert. We booked, rented, and paid for a home in the area. It was a large home, and we wanted all our children and grandchildren to come down. Meredith had tickets from Ottawa, and as Ed and I were going to be down there for five weeks, the children all planned to join us for short times.

Bruce was bringing his golf clubs and really wanted to golf with his dad in the desert. He had been there before and really liked the PGA course there. Ed and I brought our clubs along, and were so looking forward to being with all our children.

We invited our friends from the USA that were vacationing there to come over for dinner the second evening we were there. During dinner, Ed passed out, became unconscious, and slumped forward. He was seemingly all right a few minutes later.

The next day I went shopping with my girlfriends and left him watching golf on TV. When I came home, he told me that he had passed out again, so I immediately took him to Eisenhower Hospital in Palm Springs. We were there for a few hours and he was discharged as normal. The following morning, he passed out in our bedroom, so I took Ed back to the hospital and they admitted him on April 4, 2009.

In the hospital, he was going to the bathroom and he fell, hitting his head on the metal door and became unconscious. He was found with a large laceration on his forehead and a lot of blood on him. The doctors sutured his forehead. Apparently, the monitor that they had attached to Ed was not working and was faulty. Ed had also broken a finger when he fell.

Luckily, I had good medical insurance, but the insurance company told me that they wanted to air ambulance Ed back to Canada. This was now our fifth day of our five-week vacation. Our daughter Cheryl who is a critical care specialist in Kelowna was in constant touch with the hospital and me.

We notified all the children and they all cancelled their plans, as they wanted to be near their dad during this critical time. Our friends Gerry and Gloria Mudge arrived, stayed in the condo for ten days, and took over the rental car.

I went back to the condo, packed up all our possessions, left our golf clubs and other luggage with the Quasts, and hurried back to the hospital. The air ambulance arrived from San Diego, and luckily they had room for my overnight bag and me. There were three nurses and two pilots. We were sent by air to Kelowna where an ambulance was waiting to take Ed to the hospital.

He was there for a few weeks, and we came home to Abbotsford.

Subsequently, and later on, Ed was not feeling well, had a scan, and the doctor found massive bleeding in his brain. He was taken to Royal Columbian Hospital with a large brain bleed and was operated on in May 20, 2009. Ed had always worn contact lens in his eyes, but he could no longer wear them, so I got him fitted for glasses.

Ed made some recovery and in the summer of 2010 he was at his best but not well.

In June 2012, Ed tore out of the *Vancouver Sun* an ad about the Russian ballet coming to Vancouver, which was the only Canadian city on its North American tour. He said that he would like to go to it. When Cheryl asked me what I though her dad would like for his birthday and Father's Day, I mentioned this to her. She got tickets for both of us.

I must tell you that this evening at the Queen Elizabeth Theater was one of the most enjoyable evening both of us have enjoyed for a long, long time. It was totally amazing. The dancers, orchestra, and especially the sets for four acts were the best we have ever seen.

Ed probably did not follow the story as much as I did, but he loved the music and the visual. He was starting to get quite sick. We thanked Denis and Cheryl for the tickets.

Previously, Ed and I and Ernie and Ardis had tickets for the Vancouver Symphony for twenty-two years. Ed loved opera and symphony music. We really enjoyed these evenings. Occasionally, Don and Vel Kinnie joined us.

Cheryl and her husband Denis, along with Ed and Myrtle-Anne enjoying the sunshine with Cheryl's dog Tanner

CHAPTER 52

Life Now

E d recovered from his subdural hematoma but Ed later developed cortico-basal degeneration of the TAU variety with a prognosis of six to eight years after the onset of the disease. This was devastating news for me. It usually affects men from the age of around sixty to seventy years of age. There is no known cause of the disease and no cure.

Ed lost his ability to speak, read, or write very soon following the onset of this condition. It is a very rare condition. I knew that he was so frustrated with not being able to write in his journals, which he had done for fifty years.

The toll on his health was relentless and rapid. After looking after him for years in my home, I could no longer do this. Fraser Health was in touch with me, and said that I needed to put him into a care home. Well, I thought that in a few years this would be an option.

On December 25, 2014, we had an offer on our penthouse, and I decided to sell it. My breathing was so bad in the valley, as I was allergic to the grasses and farming in the area that my specialist told me that I had to relocate. So, I had decided to sell it and move to another area. I accepted the offer on December 26 and had the option of staying until May 2015.

My dilemma was that I had a sick husband, nowhere to move to, and was in a state of much uncertainty. On January 23, 2015,

Fraser Health phoned me about 8:30 in the morning to advise me that they had a placement for Ed. I was busy getting Ed ready for the day, showering, shaving him, etc., and told them that I was confident that I could look after him longer. They advised me that if I didn't take this place in Langley, I might have to wait for years.

I told them that I think I will pass and take a chance. They advised me that I had kept him at home a lot longer than I should have, which my children had also advised me.

Fraser Health asked me if I was absolutely sure, and I said yes, I would look after him.

I phoned Cheryl to tell her about the phone call. She said, "Mom, you have to take this! You have looked after him for too long." I reconsidered after talking with her, and phoned Fraser Health back an hour later, and they replied that they had already phoned someone else, and that I couldn't have it. But they said that they would call me back.

Well, they were in the process of telephoning another person, but hadn't gotten through yet, so they cancelled the call and called me back to say that the placement was secured for Ed. I was to have him there the next day. I asked if I could have two days, and when I took him there, I really cried.

Langley Lodge was not like our penthouse. Even though I had help in, and nurses, I couldn't rest. I was awake a lot at night and so tired and worn out that I knew it was for the best.

I was devastated to leave him there. I also knew that if he fell, that I could not get him up at home. Ed did have a fall shortly after I admitted him, and they needed four nurses and a gurney to get him up.

He has a lovely private room, with his own full bathroom and a nice view of the gardens. I put all his memorabilia and his awards on the walls of the room, to make it look more like his office and home.

So, he is living there now, and has become very disabled. He is content, not in any pain, and lives in the moment. But this has been the hardest thing I have ever done in my life. He is such a good person, classy, and a gentle soul.

Now, I had three months to downsize from a 3,100 square foot penthouse to find a place in Vancouver. We found a small apartment in the Yale town area of Vancouver, renovated it all to my comfort and taste, and I am living there now. I moved in about May 15, 2015.

When Ed first got sick, we heard a lovely song that Jim Brady wrote and sang. It has become very precious to me It is called

Every Cry is Heard

When you face life's great disappointments
And answers are so hard to find
There is One you can always depend on
To walk every step by your side
Every cry is heard by the Father
Not one tear from your eye goes unseen
He lovingly cares for His children
Let His love be the strength that you need

There's a deep settled peace when you know Him
You can rest just knowing He cares
No matter what's waiting before you
He has promised He'll always be there

CHAPTER 53

Leaving Town Centre Tower

I loved our penthouse. I had my own studio in the loft that over-looked the whole apartment. Ed had a lovely gentlemen's office right off the front entrance to the apartment, and we had the most incredible three hundred-degree views of the valley and the mountains. Our place was air-conditioned, had four fireplaces with the bedroom fireplace going into the bathroom. It was so lovely with many large patios.

We had lots of parking and storage. But, most of all, I knew I would miss my friends and neighbors in the building as well as the residents of Abbotsford. We had lived in this penthouse for twen-ty-one years, the longest that we had ever lived in one place. Even now, sometimes I have regrets for selling it, but I knew my health was more important, and it did feel like a large mausoleum without Ed there.

I knew that I had to move, because my asthma was so bad in the valley. My parents both had asthma, so I inherited adult-onset asthma. The valley was not good for me.

So, Cheryl and I found a small suite in Vancouver, and I decided to move into it. It is in Yaletown beside False Creek.

Now, I had to downsize, and as my friends can attest, it was a humongous job. Firstly, I tackled my studio. I got rid of lots of old pieces, college plates that I used for printmaking, old paints, and framing supplies. It took me about a week to get rid of most of the items.

Next I tackled Ed's office.

This was where the hub of Ed's life was. It was my most difficult time on downsizing.

Luckily, Derek wanted to take Ed's desk and green leather chair. Ed had this desk since the company moved to its head office on Bourquin Street, and he was so fond of this large mahogany desk with a green leather top and spent many, many hours at it.

When we had the home office in our apartment, he would go there right after breakfast, make phone calls, do office work, and would have a time when he would pray and memorize scripture. I think he memorized about one hundred scriptures and where they were found. He felt that this was a great way to keep his mind active. I always knew when he was doing this, as he would close his door to the office and wanted to be left alone.

Ed had an unbelievable faith in God, and loved his family unconditionally. He never focused on the problems of members of his family but worked on a solution to every challenge that was presented to him.

Ed also wrote in his notebook, which he took to every meeting he went to, along with his cell phone, his briefcase, and his date-timer. Ed had a ring binder notebook that he wrote in everyday. He put the date at the top of the page and recorded every phone call, any meeting that he attended and every conversation that he had.

When I looked at our storage, there was two "bankers boxes" of notebooks written on both sides of the page. He also had a prayer journal

During these years, Ed was on many boards of governors, which included:

- Canadian Board of the Robert Schuler Ministries
- Board of Elders of the Sevenoaks Alliance Church (Finance Committee)
- Board of Governors of BCIT

- President of the BC Concrete Assn.
- President of the Canadian Amalgamated Construction Association
- Member of the Economic Development Advisory board for the City of Abbotsford
- Board of Governors for the Matsqui Police Commission
- Member of the United Way Association
- Member of the BC Tax Assessment Board.
- Board of Governors of the Youth for Christ organization.
- Founding President of the ICBA
- President of the former Abbotsford Social Credit Assn.

There are others I don't recall as well.

Ed did a lot of business in this office, some of the partnerships he had and worked on in this office were:

- Cheam Holdings with Henry Matties and Stan Hindmarsh
- Annop Kholsa in Lower Mainland Steel and Lower Mainland concrete products
- Don Quast in Abbotsford Hyundai
- John Voth—Town Center Tower
- Colin Regan—Eco-Hydro Energy
- Dennis Neumann and Jake Klaassen—Fraser River Resources
- Larry Fisher—various enterprises
- Dave Walden—Rempel Bros. Concrete Inc. and Greenbank Sand and Gravel
- Lakeside Concrete Ltd.
- Apollo Concrete Products
- Sandy Key Investments Ltd.
- Sandy Key Investments (US) Ltd.
- Sandy Key Developments Ltd.
- Sandy Key Automotive Ltd.

So, as you can imagine, I had a hard time closing down his lovely office with thousands of books and many files. I systematically went through it and shredded all files that were more than seven years old. I also went through the storage and shredded all papers that were older than seven years. It was quite emotional to do this, but it had to be done.

I told everyone that I met to come and get as many books that they wanted. The buyers said that they would take any books that were left.

I told my kids, grandkids, and all family members to come and get anything they wanted. Kirk took a lot, as he didn't have much furniture or bedding.

I was really lucky that so many people came to my place and offered to buy large pieces of furniture that I knew I would not have room for. Also, my brother-in-law, Glenn Follis, who was a minister, took most of Ed's clothes. Luckily, he was the exact same size as Ed and didn't have to alter anything. Ed had so many expensive pieces of clothing, as he really liked to dress well. Bruce took a few sweaters and other items.

Lots of small items were given away, and I was left with almost an empty penthouse, which allowed me to just take things that I really wanted and had room for in my small apartment in Vancouver. It actually felt good to get rid of a lot of "stuff" and I found it "freeing."

CHAPTER 54

My Board Involvements

I have always enjoyed working on various boards. When we first moved to Abbotsford, I served on the Christian Women's Club along with some of my friends Ardis Janzen, Alvina Klassen, Doris Wiebe, and many others. It was a fun time. I think I was on it about three years. We did some traveling with the board.

I also was part of the Junior Hospital Auxiliary Board for the Abbotsford Hospital. I mainly worked in the shop on the main floor where we sold flowers, homemade knitted items, candy, etc.

I served on the Mill Lake Steering Committee, which was looking into the possibility of getting an arts center to be built in Abbotsford.

Ardis and Ernie and Ed and I attended the Vancouver Symphony Orchestra concerts for twenty-two years. When Ernie got sick, we slowed down on attending. A new symphony was being formed in Abbotsford, so I went on the board of the Fraser Valley Symphony and served for about five years on that. Ardis also later joined us until the symphony could no longer afford to pay the players and it was disbanded.

In the late '90s, Gerry Charles phoned me that they were going to start a charity called the Crystal Gala. She invited ladies to join her. It started off with just a few members and has been ongoing for eighteen years. After a few years, we made it into a foundation and it is now called the Crystal Gala Foundation. It is a marvelous organization of girls, who sit around the kitchen table and plan a fundraiser every year for breast cancer. The event, held in October of each year, is always sold out early. I was thrilled to join the other ladies in our community who put all this effort into a fun gala. Every lady pays her own way and expense so that every dollar raised is used for breast cancer. We have raised over two million dollars and the funds stay in the community in which we have established a Crystal Gala Breast Cancer Unit in the lobby of the Abbotsford Regional Hospital and Cancer Center.

We were finally able to get a professional class A gallery in Abbotsford. In 2008, Milt Walker phoned me and asked if I would sit on the board of governors of this new gallery. I was delighted. We chose the name Reach Gallery Museum Abbotsford.

It was a challenge to get it up and running and I was pleased to be appointed to this wonderful board. We get exhibits from all over the world. Our residents often would not be able to see these exhibits, if we would not have showcased them in this class A gallery. It is a marvelous jewel in the center of the city properties.

Cheryl Raabe, Emily Voth, Alvina Klassen,
Elaine Funk, Sheryl Quast
(Girls Birthday lunch at my place)

CHAPTER 55

Living in Vancouver

My apartment is near the water, and it affords me the ability to walk everywhere. I find that I walk to all my appointments and put many miles going to and fro from everywhere. It is a great life style and I am making more and more friends in Vancouver.

I have become really good friends with Hank and Elaine Funk who have a place in the building right beside mine, and have been incredibly good to me.

I see Ardis and Norm Friesen a lot, as we still have live theater play tickets for the season each year. They are so good to me and their home in Abbotsford is always open to me.

Roman and Lori Sosnowski have an apartment in Vancouver, and I see them often. They also have a home in West Kelowna and I spend some Christmases with them.

My cousin Ruth and her husband Peter Klassen get together with me often. They live in the White Rock area of Surrey. They both are so kind to me. Ruth is my cousin, and her and I have become closer these past few years. They are wonderful people. They visit me often

Ed and Edith Toews often meet up with me when attending the Canadian Gospel concerts in Red Deer, Alberta. It is always lovely to re-connect with them since they moved to White Rock from Fort St. John. Ed and my Ed have always been such good friends.

John and Emily Voth have their yacht moored in False Creek and I see them often.

I have reconnected with other friends from Abbotsford who live in Vancouver also, including Mark and Darlene Johnson, Ursula Jones, Sandy Regehr, and others. Mark Johnson was Ed's and my tax accountant for years, so it was lovely to reconnect with him and Darlene.

My breathing has improved significantly and I am seeing some very good specialists. I have found out that I had huge allergies to the farming in the valley and the pollution that blows into the valley from the city.

*Ardis and Norm Friesen-Roman and lori
Sosnowski—friends for dinner.*

CHAPTER 56

Bruce

Bruce was working in the US at our concrete and gravel operation. He was there for about eleven years. My partner, Dave Walden, and he ran the company.

He had a very difficult time visiting Ed in the home. When he was coming through to go to Kelowna, he would often stop and see Ed. He would always cry when he saw him. It really affected Bruce a lot that his dad, whom he called his best friend, was going to die in the next six years. He was inconsolable a lot of the time.

Bruce lived in a beautiful sub-penthouse in the Dolphins building in Kelowna. He loved all things Kelowna, waterskiing, skiing, and just the lifestyle there.

He was instrumental in getting 100 acres of the 165 acres we have on Whidbey Island where our business is located, rezoned for gravel.

He would work down there for about ten days, then come home to Kelowna for ten days, and drive back to the USA. I know this was hard on him. He had high blood pressure, and did not have a healthy lifestyle.

I knew that Bruce had a lot of angst in his life, and I often wondered if it was the fact that he was adopted, even though he loved his dad and I so much. He wrote beautiful letters to Ed and I on Mother's Day and Father's Day that would bring us to tears.

When he was in Kelowna, he spent a lot of his time with his girls. On February 11, 2016, his daughter Alyssa phoned me to ask if I had heard from her dad. He was going to pick her up from school, take her to dinner, and to a movie.

When he didn't show up, she started to text me and phoning me. I checked with the garage where his truck was being repaired to see if his vehicle was still there. They were closed but when I checked first thing in the morning, it was still there. I had been thinking that maybe he made a hurried trip to the US.

Alyssa and I talked all evening and were very worried about him. My last text from Bruce was at about 2:30 PM. He told me that he wanted to take Alyssa to Kenya in the future as visiting this country had made a huge difference in his life.

Cheryl was in Toronto, so I phoned her to ask if she could go and check on him as soon as she arrived home at 8 am the next morning. She had the only FOB and key for his apartment.

When she arrived home, she went directly there, and sent a text to me: "GET ON A PLANE AND COME ASAP." I called her and she told me he was comatose and that the medics were trying to revive him. He was cold and had been lying there for probably sixteen hours. She thought he was dead.

I tried to fly out right away from Vancouver. My friends Ardis and Norm Friesen took me to the airport, and I tried to get a plane out, but all the airlines were totally booked. A nice West Jet supervisor helped me to get a taxi and I took the bus to Kelowna arriving at midnight and Cheryl took me directly to the hospital.

Bruce was hooked up to so many machines, including breathing. He was comatose most of the time. I stayed with him for the next ten days, mostly all day. Dear Cheryl was on ICU on the most strenuous and busy ten-day shift she has done for a long time.

It was very emotional time and on February 22, 2016, ten days later, Bruce passed away at fifty-two years of age. He was diagnosed with complications from a massive stroke with many smaller strokes. He was not a healthy person, and did not look after his health. His lungs were not working and he developed acute pneumonia.

We had a lovely memorial service for him on a boat on the Okanagan Lake from which we could see his apartment. He was cremated and we put a few ashes in the lake. It was the way Alyssa wanted it to happen.

Cheryl was so amazing. She organized the whole thing. It was such a beautiful day. The day before and the day after the service, it was blustery on the lake, but this day was absolutely beautiful. Just as we put a few ashes in the water, a beautiful rainbow came out.

It was a beautiful time. There were about fifty of us present. Lots of family, cousins, and special friends attended. Kirk, as well as his daughter, Shae-Lynn, was there. Kirk was very emotional.

Glenn Follis did a beautiful job of giving some remarks and prayers. Derek gave a beautiful eulogy. He lived with Bruce for a while and knew him well. It was Easter Saturday.

We had appetizers, looked at photo albums, and remembered with fondness Bruce.

After the service and during this time of sadness, Cheryl and I had to empty and clean his apartment so that the owner could take immediate possession. Cheryl was the executor of the estate and it was a huge job to sell his collectables, etc.

Bruce used to talk to his father every day when he was down in the US and I would often hear them laughing on the phone. Since Ed has been sick, he called me quite often to chat with me and apprise me about what was going on in our company there. I am so thankful that Dave Walden, my partner down there, is taking over the business. He calls me quite often and discusses our plans for the businesses.

Also during this time, this lovely little girl Alyssa, while grieving her father, was graduating from high school at the age of seventeen. Cheryl and I both went to her "grad walk" and her graduation ceremony. I am so very proud of her. She told me that she wanted to honor her dad by taking the best parts of him and making him proud of her and she is certainly doing that.

I am so thankful that this happened when he was at home in Kelowna and not on the road he traveled every ten days, nor the time he was working in the USA.

Bruce's Eulogy

Rempel, Edward BruceBruce was born 25 January, 1964, died all too soon on February 22, 2016, in Kelowna, B. C. Bruce was a family man, devoted to his loving daughters, Alyssa and Samantha, and Alyssa's best friend Ali (Shrimp) Lea. He will be missed dearly by his sister, Cheryl Holmes, brother Kirk Rempel, mother Myrtle-Ann Rempel, father Edward Rempel, nephew Derek Holmes, nieces Meredith Holmes and Shae-Lynn Rempel. We will all remember him for his kindness and sense of humour, especially on the golf course. Bruce loved all things Kelowna; skiing, tennis, hockey, water-skiing, listening to rock music, and just hanging out with his daughters. The family is grateful for the exemplary care he received in his final days at Kelowna General Hospital ICU, and gifts in his memory can be made to the Kelowna Hospital Foundation.

Cheryl Holmes

Bruce.

Bruce and his daughter Samantha Dawn
at her High School graduation

Bruce's youngest daughter - Alyssa Ann - 2017

CHAPTER 57

My Art Career

I mentioned that my favorite course in school was always art from the time I was little. For the high school annual, I even did a few cartoon characters. So when we were living on Woodbine Street, I saw an ad about a lady named Gladys Murray who gave drawing lessons. I took a few of them, and noticed that the University of the Fraser Valley offered an art degree. It was then called Fraser Valley College.

I enrolled in it and met my friend Gerry Thompson, who was also enrolled. It took me four years as I was doing it part time under the tutelage of Mircho and Janena Jakabow.

I started from the basics drawing, painting, mostly from live models and doing lithography. I also studied art history, sculpture, and ceramics. A famous man named John Weaver taught the sculpture course. He was so talented.

I loved working with my hands, but hated the casting of the sculptures, so I concentrated on art history and painting. I also did some courses on psychology and did a minor in accounting, which came so easily to me. Probably from all the years I did bookkeeping.

I graduated in 1986 with a major in painting (hon.) and a minor in accounting.

The university didn't offer a BFA at that time, or I would have continued, but even though I didn't need it, I continued doing more courses to get as much information as I could. I have always said that I have a "thirst for learning." I love to learn about new things. The Jakabows were very influential in my art career. I also studied with many other artists those years.

During the four years, that I was studying, I took two years of printmaking, which included lithography, and silkscreen. I also took art history, which became one of the most important courses that I have ever taken.

Later on, during my travels to Europe, etc., it was such a helpful course. During my years at college, I took some trips with the group to various places. Gerry Thompson also was on many of these trips.

On one trip, Gerry, Ed, and I went to Pennsylvania to visit her in-laws. This was a fun experience. Gerry is a marvelous painter in watercolors and has become very successful.

We went to San Francisco to visit art galleries and also went to a papermaking place. We went to so many various sculpture and other museums.

On one of the trips we took was to New York City with the class. Ed accompanied me on this trip and it was one of the most exciting places that we had ever visited.

New York City was not very safe for pedestrians on the street then, so we walked in groups in the evening to visit the theaters, etc. Later on, Rudy Giuliani became mayor and it became the safest large city in America.

When we arrived in New York, we went to our hotel. When we turned on the lights, we heard scurrying and Ed was so upset. We arrived at about two AM so Ed called the manager and said that he was not going to stay in the same room as whatever was there. So the manager told us that he would move us to the top floor which had really been redone. We made sure we kept our suitcases zipped up and slept for a few hours until we were meeting the group in the morning. Ed wanted to change hotels, but I didn't want to feel that we were being snobbish, so I told him we should just be careful.

The next morning Janina told us that cockroaches were in the whole hotel, and our room wasn't immune from it. We stayed there for five days, went to a fashion house, and had a great time. Ed and I walked a lot until late at night, slept for a few hours, and didn't spend any time in our room.

Later on, I checked out ratings for hotels in Manhattan. I found out that it wasn't the worst hotel in Manhattan, it was the second worst hotel.

Our next trip to Manhattan, we stayed at the beautiful Plaza Hotel, that Donald Trump owned, and were offered a lovely suite with a fireplace as an upgrade with a very great price. Later on, Ed and I took many trips to New York. We both enjoyed live theater so much as well as visiting all the art galleries.

I graduated from the University of the Fraser Valley in 1986, with a major in painting (hon.).

I went to Cannon Beach, Oregon, one year to spend a week painting the coast of Oregon. I painted on Salt Spring Island with some senior artists and also went to Myrtle Beach one year to paint for two weeks.

I painted in oils for years, landscapes, ocean scenes, etc. Then I did portraits for years, and did my three children and my grand-mother as well as many others.

I then painted flowers and foliage in oils, but found that I wanted to loosen up, so I started to paint watercolors and paint "wet on wet" to try to put more emotion into my work. I must have painted hundreds of flowers, and I say now, that if I never paint another flower, I would be happy.

After that period, I started in acrylics and then did mixed media. This process is done with pieces of paper that I paint on and affix to my paintings to get the emotion I would like. This is a process far harder than copying a still life, or a portrait, as it totally evolves one's emotions being expressed. I often use 14K gold leaf under my work to give it more luminosity.

I have experienced some measure of success, as I have obtained four signature designations, which are very difficult to obtain: Associate of the federation Gallery (AFCA), Senior Federation

Canada assn. (SFCA) Northwest Watercolor Society (NWWS), and Canadian Society of Painters in Watercolor (CSPWC).

I did serve as vice-president of the Federation Gallery for a few years. The gallery was started by Lauren Harris seventy-five years ago. I just participated in a seventy-fifth anniversary show for signature artists where I had the pleasure of showing a piece of my work.

I do donate a lot of my work to charity.

My artwork is all over the world, Ireland, the USA, Europe, and Africa.

You can visit my website artist.ca/mrempel Myrtle-Anne Rempel, SFCA, NWWS, CSPWC (Google to see a resume).

"Mixed Media Painting Impression of mom's dating year"

Abstract painting of Impression of my mom

CHAPTER 58

Our Cars

E d and I always liked nice cars. He had a really nice car when I met him. He and his buddies in Abbotsford would always customize their cars and ride around the city, usually meeting at their friend Jake Siemens's garage.

Later, when we could afford it, we bought the two brand new cars that I totaled in the car accidents. We especially liked Jaguars. I could probably write a book on our experiences with these cars. It was a love-hate relationship with them in the early days. Ed used to tell me that his Jag was like me in some ways. It was beautiful, comfortable, and so nice to sit in, but once in a while it would do something really stupid. It usually had to do with the electrical system. We would both laugh.

We had a Honda Civic that we bought for Cheryl for her sixteenth birthday to travel to Trinity University in Langley. She got engaged to Barry, so we bought it from her. We gave it to Bruce for his sixteenth birthday, but he bought another car, so we bought it from him. In the meantime, he and a friend rolled it, so it cost us almost as much as the car was worth to fix it. We sold it to my brother, but it caused him so much trouble that we bought it back. It finally stopped on the highway, and we towed it to the auto wrecker's yard. We think we paid for that car about six times. We had a lot of laughs over that.

When Cheryl graduated from high school, her friend and her took our old 1948 MGTC convertible for the graduation.

Ed also bought his favorite beautiful 1980-308 red Ferrari, of which he got a little bit of money from his family's estate. We paid the difference. We also had some Mercedes convertibles.

We had other cars as well. The last beautiful gift that Ed gave me just before Ed got sick was a gorgeous candy apple red Jaguar convertible with a tan interior. I really liked that car. Now, I just drive a Lexus SUV.

A funny story happened when Ed was in charge of our company building the Expo 86 project. He was driving back and forth to Vancouver from Abbotsford at least once a day. He often didn't realize how fast he was going as the Jag was so smooth.

He got a lot of speeding tickets. One day when he was driving from North Vancouver to Abbotsford, his brother-in-law, Rev. Glenn Follis, accompanied him. As they were driving down the hill, a siren went on. Uh-oh. Ed said to Glenn, "I can't get another ticket, and maybe I should make a run for it." Poor Glenn could just see it. "Pastor Breaking the Law along with His Brother-in-Law" in the news.

Well, they stopped and Ed later got a letter taking away his license for a month. The problem was, now I had to drive him every day to Vancouver. He would ask me to park a block away from the office so his staff wouldn't know. Then when he was ready to go to Vancouver, I would pick him up and drive him into the city. It was the time when he was really involved in the Expo 86 project.

Well, me not being a good driver, he would comment all the way. "Get in the left lane," "Don't hit the potholes." etc. One day after we got over the Port Mann Bridge, I stopped the car and said, "I have my license and you don't so if you don't like it you can walk." Well, that lasted for about half an hour and then it started again. I was sure glad when he got his license back. Bruce told his dad that he was being penalized twice for having to have Mom drive him. Later we had lots of laughs about that.

CHAPTER 59

Letters from My Children, Who Have Blessed My Life So Much

C heryl Holmes—(she kept her married name when she got all her degrees) has such a beautiful home in Kelowna overlooking the lake, in which she has fixed up a beautiful suite for Ed and I. I get to enjoy it on my frequent trips to Kelowna.

She is an amazing girl with a heart of gold, so caring, and so smart. I am so blessed to have her in my life. I love her so much. She calls me Sista as neither her nor I have a sister, so we have become so close and talk almost every day and sometimes more often. She is my best friend and I don't know what I would do without her in my life. I thank God every day that He gave her to us.

This is a letter she wrote to me on December 19, 2014.

Dear Mom,

On your birthday, I have been reflecting back on your extraordinary life. It began twenty-two years before mine and I am thinking how different your early life was than mine. You grew up in a household where you had a lot of responsibility—I had practically none. You had six robust brothers to contend with and I had only two. You were not praised for your accomplishments and received no encouragement to pursue your dreams, and I was. You were not told you were pretty or smart, and you were not made to feel special in any way. I was—by my parents, my uncles, and my teachers. After me, your early life was filled with pain and isolation. You worked extremely hard to enable my dad's dreams and received little or no support and harbored a lot of guilt where mothers nowadays have little. You quietly bore society's expectations of you and balanced the needs of your family and your husband with little or no thought to your own. It seems unreal to me how privileged my life has been and you remain so supportive of me despite my unintentionally strong self-concept. Thanks to you, I have experienced life that has had no limits or boundaries to my dreams and I recognize that yours has had many limits imposed on you and still you shine. I can't take any credit. All the credit goes to God for giving you to me as a Mother, a nurturer and a friend.

Mom, you are extraordinary. God has given you so many gifts that run parallel to your sorrows; gifts of humility, empathy, and deep, deep emotional beauty.

On your birthday, Mom, I want to tell you that you are in my thoughts and prayers all day. I am praying that God will bless you with peace and contentment and great hope. That He will give you a little bit of Heaven now on this Earth and that you will have no worry or angst for the future. You are enough. You are perfect.

Love, Cher.

Kirk is such an amazing son. I call him my "joy child." He lights up a room when he comes in. He is so helpful to me and to everyone he knows. He is generous to a fault. Always giving to friends. If I need anything he is always there for me.

We are all grieving my son Bruce and go through periods of "waves of sadness" but life goes on. Bruce was especially close to his dad, but every Mother's Day, he would send me a lovely letter. I will enclose just one of his letters, sent in 2014. I feel so humbled to get these letters. He also sent me lovely letters on my birthday. They are so precious to me.

Hi Mom

Well, here I am trying to figure out how to put such strong feelings into a mix of letters and sentences that in no way can actually express my true admiration for you. As most Mother's Days, I'm reminded once again how much my life could have not have not been so positively altered had you not been there on a day in January fifty years ago. Having you as a mother was the best thing that ever has and ever will be the best thing to ever happen to me. I can't thank you enough for every-thing you do, everything you have done, and all you do in the future. I got so lucky that you stepped in as my mother so long ago. I am a true believer that there is no such a thing as fate and people make their own outcome. That said to end up in your hands being only a few days old I would guess could only be just that only word that works. I got so lucky.

I would like to thank you for all you continually do daily, weekly, and all throughout the year. I couldn't imagine life without your help. I cannot imagine how I would get through life without you, period.

This Mother's Day, however, it's dawned on me that this isn't just about you being my mother, but also my appreciation and admiration for what you do for Dad. Once again, a jumble of letters put into sentences on a piece of paper just don't do justice to express my admira-tion for how you care for and deal with Dad. I wish there was so much more I could to help but there you are every day caring for him. You know how much he means and has meant to me in my life. The challenges you face on behalf of all of the family are truly many and how you handle them with such poise and calmness is incredible. You truly are the "rock" in this family. There is no way we could survive this without you. We are nothing without you! All the money in the world could not replace what you do for us and especially me.

Thank you!

So, this isn't just a Happy Mother's Day wish, it's a Happy All You Do Day. I don't know how you've done it or how you do it but I'm extremely fortunate that somehow, someday I ended up with you for a mother.

I love and appreciate you so much. Happy Mother's Day.

Bruce

The following is a note that Kirk sent me for my birthday in December 2016. He sent it with a lot of computer expressions.

HAPPY BIRTHDAY. I thought I would send you something that would put a smile on your face. I thank you so much for raising me right. It's wonderful to have the most incredible memories. You've shown me and taught me a lot. I couldn't have wished for a more perfect mother. Thank you, and I love you.

Your Joy Child

I am the luckiest, most blessed person to have had these three children in my life.

CHAPTER 60

2016-2017

I am also planning on a few trips.

I went to Palm Desert in November 2016 for about two weeks. I visited my brother Murray and his wife Ingrid, my cousin Darlene and her husband Paul, my good friends Dr. Gary and Laurie Siemens and all the Abbotsford people that vacation there. It was so much fun. Elaine and Hank had a great American Thanksgiving dinner down there, with many friends and including the Baergs who bought our penthouse in Abbotsford, Don and Sheryl Quast hosted me a few times also. I stayed at the Embassy Suites in La Quinta, so it was convenient to visit everyone.

I really want to go to see my really good friend Mikki Engelman who lives in Mesa, Arizona, with her husband Paul. She and I have been such good buddies for over forty years. We talk often. She was my prayer partner for a few years when we were going through a few trying times.

We used to go for lunch after we prayed, and one day we came out of a prayer time, we noticed a bird had done his business on her windshield. She said to me, "A bird shat on my car." I said to her, "What does that word mean?" She said, "Have you heard of the 'past tense' word?" We have had a lot of laughs over the years. Mikki is so funny and she brings so much laughter in my life, even though sometimes she uses phrases that are a bit salty.

Later on, I did some prayer and lunches with a good friend Carol Reddicopp before she moved to Cultus Lake.

Last Photo of Myrtle-Anne and Ed.

Postscript

As I finish this memoir, I just want to say how very thankful I am for so many things. I am so very grateful for good health, for the lovely place I live in, for the ability to walk every day for miles if I so choose. I am so grateful for family, for my wonderful friends, who include me in so many of their activities.

God has been very good to me. I know Ed's passing is on the horizon, but that is ok. I know he is going to a better place. A huge thank you to everyone who has been so special to Ed and myself. I may have gotten some facts slightly wrong and I hope you will be forgiving.

"Do not fear, for I am your God. I will strengthen you and help you; I will uphold you with My righteous right hand". Isaiah 41:10

A 19th-century theologian, Charles Spurgeon wrote "Now contentment is one of the flowers of heaven, and it must be cultivated".

I have learned to be content whatever the circumstances but it hasn't always been easy for me.

I am looking forward to what God has planned for my life in the future. It is an exciting time to be alive. Each day that I wake up, I look out of my window and say, "This is the day that the Lord has made, and I will be glad in it."

Painting in Red

About the Author

Myrtle-Anne Rempel is a grateful person for all the good things that have happened in her life, but also thankful for the challenges she faced to help her better understand what others are facing. She studied interior design, but is now involved with the visual arts. She finds the challenges of her paintings to be the passion that drives her to fulfill her innermost desires. Her collections are featured in many countries in the world. You may read about her if visit artists.ca/mrempel. She loves her family dearly, and is thankful for many great friendships.

Education

- ○ Studied—New York School of Interior Design, 1972
- ○ University of the Fraser Valley (Honors), Best Painting of the Year Award; Graduated 1986
- ○ Studied with many great teachers—including Mircko Jakobow, and Allan Edwards

MYRTLE—ANNE REMPEL SFCA, CSPWC, NWWS

Myrtle-Anne graduated from the University of the Fraser Valley with a major in Painting and Printmaking (Honors). She has exhibited extensively and has won many awards in Canada and the USA. Including the ARTY award for outstanding visual artist. She is frequently asked to jury art in Vancouver and the Fraser Valley.

October 8th, 2014—at the 40th Anniversary of the UFV, Myrtle-Anne received the honor of being one of the "40 Distinguished

Alumni "for excellence in public service, business, the environment and service to the community.

She was awarded signature status in the Federation of Canadian Artists.—2000 AFCA, and in 2003 SFCA, She was also awarded signature status with the Can. Society of Painters in Watercolor in 2001 (CSPWC) and the North West Watercolor Society (NWWS) in 2012. Her work is included in many private, corporate and Government collections in Canada, USA, Ireland, Austria, France, China and Africa.

Myrtle-Anne was asked by the Prime Minister of Ireland to hang her painting titled "Butterflies in Belfast": in their permanent collection in Government House in Dublin. This Painting depicts a symbol of Hope for lasting peace & reconciliation.

She has been featured in many publications including:

Artist of BC, Art Impressions, Country Living, Focus Newspaper, The Abbotsford Times, the Abbotsford News, (six feature articles) and the Federation of Canadian Artists cover (4 times),

2014 POTE Dossier, UFV, 40th Anniversary Magazine.

She did two commissions for the Cover of the Alliance Women annual magazines for their International Publications.

She previously worked as an Interior Designer. Her community work includes serving on the board of the Crystal Gala Foundation for Breast cancer, serving on the board of governors of the Federation of Canadian Artists, and serving on the board of Governors of the Reach Gallery Museum since its inauguration.

She may be reached at sandykey@me.com—or telephone 1-604-309-3995 Website artists.ca/mrempel—Myrtle-Anne Rempel, SFCA. NWWS, CSPWC

CPSIA information can be obtained
at www.ICGtesting.com
Printed in the USA
LVHW07s1239140518
576509LV00004B/7/P